How to Get the Most Out of College

127 Ways to Make Connections, Make it Work for You, and Make a Difference

Elliot Felix

¶

Alinea Learning

Boston

Alinea Learning

Boston, Massachusetts

Published in the United States by Alinea Learning, an imprint and division of Alinea Knowledge, LLC, Boston.

Visit our website at www.alinealearning.com.

Library of Congress Cataloging-in-Publication Data is available on file.

Print paperback ISBN: 978-1-7358107-6-8

eBook ISBN: 978-1-7358107-7-5

For Nora and Theo.

When you two enter college in the 2030s, I hope you find college even better than it is today – a place where you can each find your people, your purpose, and your path toward it.

Between now and then, I also hope this book will have helped students create their best college experience and helped institutions offer affordable access, inspiring classes, research that makes a difference, and inclusive communities set in remarkable places.

Contents

Preface

Your experience in college isn't something you navigate or get through. It's more than an obstacle course, though it can sometimes feel like one. It's an experience you create so you can get the most out of college. You make it work for you so you have the information, inspiration, and support you need. You make connections with people, to places, and between ideas. You make a difference.

Your college or university's role is to provide opportunities and support. Your role is to be intentional and focused to capitalize on what college offers to create your best experience. You are in charge. You are making it happen. This book is a field guide to show you how with 127 tips that are the building blocks you need to create a great college experience. And although every college and every student are different, you can apply these ideas wherever you go.

My Mission: Making Schools Better for Students

Since I was a student, making colleges better has been important to me. When I was in student government at the University of Virginia as an undergrad and then MIT for grad school, I helped students have a voice, connect classrooms to careers, and increase affordability and pay. In addition, I spotlighted students' work. This work is so important to me that I started an education consulting company with a mission to make college more engaging and equitable.

Working with passionate and knowledgeable people with backgrounds in design, research, and business, we helped improve the student experience at over a hundred colleges and universities by improving their student services, their campuses, and their technology. Working with this great team, I've had the chance to conduct more than two thousand interviews, focus groups, workshops, and town hall meetings with students, faculty, staff, and university leaders – plus surveys of many more. I've learned a lot from all these conversations and our research along the way.

Sharing What I've Learned from Working with more than One Hundred Colleges

Now I want to share what I've learned about how colleges work so that you can get the most out of your experience and be better connected to your courses, campus, community, and career. Because opportunities to make the most of college haven't always been equally available to all students, the insights in this book can help level the playing field so that everyone has the chance to learn, grow, belong, and succeed.

Seeing your education as something you create is so important. One student I interviewed put it best:

> *When you go to college, you can let the curriculum, the instructors, and the administrators decide. But then you are only going to have the experience they intend you to have. You are giving them a lot of power. When you take on the autonomy of designing your own experience – on your own terms – you advocate for yourself and your needs in and out of the classroom. Then the experience will be so much more than it would be otherwise. We all deserve to have an experience that celebrates who we are. This only happens if you decide to design it.*

As I thought about the hundreds of projects I've done with colleges and universities, I realized there are four common ways I've helped students learn, grow, and belong:

- By enabling students to more meaningfully interact with each other and their professors in and out of the classroom
- By bringing together the services that support students into hubs so that these services are more visible, accessible, and effective
- By supporting students' projects that make an impact on the world and on their own lives (by showing them their purpose and career path)
- By creating environments and events that welcome people and create diverse, dynamic places

These are the kinds of experiences and environments that I hope all students can create with some help from this book. This book can be used as a practical "field guide" to college.

The book contains **127** short tips on how to design your college experience that are based on my work with more than a hundred colleges and universities, my interviews with a variety of experts and students, and my research into what works and why – research that you can dig into yourself by reading the notes at the end of each chapter if you want to learn more.

By combining what I've learned from talking to a diverse set of students and experts with evidence about what works and what doesn't from hundreds of research studies, I will show you how to get the most out of college.

Each short tip is a kind of building block you can use to create your college experience. Each has a few sentences about what to do, the research behind why to do it, and suggestions and stories on how to do it. It's also important that you hear not only from experts but from other students as well.

Beyond the what, why, and how to make the most of college, there are stories from students throughout the book (in italics) on what worked for them and what did not so that you can hear from other students directly. Most of these stories came from my interviews with students, but when I read about a student's experience that fit perfectly with a tip, I included it and cited the source so you can read more.

You don't have to read all the tips in order. You can skip around. You don't even have to read all the tips. You can focus on the ones that interest you, at least to start with. And you don't have to worry or feel bad if you can't act on all the advice in here. If you can put a few tips to use, you'll have made a good start on taking charge of your education, making college work for you, and getting the most out of it.

How to Use this Book

The book is organized into three sections: (1) what you need to know about yourself and college before you go, (2) general advice for all students, and (3) advice to meet specific student needs and identities – which everyone can read because a tip for one type of student can often help another and help us better understand each other.

Foundational Advice on Your College Experience

Because your college experience is complex, the general advice covers the six core parts of your experience: classes, support services, environment, technology, relationships, and career. Considering these different aspects holistically is crucial, because when students don't succeed, it's usually not because of academics but because of other things going on in their lives. For instance, by some estimates nearly four in ten students who drop out of college do so for financial reasons;[1] one study found that college students with depression are twice as likely to drop out;[2] and another study found that students who don't feel a sense of belonging are less likely to graduate.[3]

Specific Advice for Different Student Identities

Because your identity is complex and intersectional, the specific advice covers a range of characteristics and needs, aimed at student-athletes, students with children, students of color, students with disabilities, first-generation college students, international students, LGBTQ+ students, transfer students, and veteran students. Of course, many students fit more than one of these profiles. In the tips targeting these different identities, you'll hear from students and experts who share these characteristics, people whose research and lived experience can help you learn, grow, and belong. Neither these identities nor the tips are comprehensive, but they are a start.

Using this Book in the Way that Works for You

Use this book in the way that works for you. You may want to read it cover to cover to get an overview and flag tips with Post-its to come back to. You may want to look at the table of contents and jump to specific sections or tips. No matter how you use it, these tips can be building blocks you assemble to make the best college experience for you. You may want to read it on your own or read it with a friend you can discuss it with. It's up to you. Each chapter has an activity to help you reflect and apply what you've been reading that's based on research into how we form good habits.[4] The good news is you've already taken the first intentional step in designing your college experience. Keep it up!

How Chapters are Organized

Here's how section two of the book is organized, with a chapter on each aspect of your college experience so you can thrive in classes, feel supported, build relationships, master technology, enjoy the campus, and explore career paths.

How Tips are Organized

Here's how a typical tip is organized so that you can get the most out of it by learning what to do, why to do it based on the research, suggestions on how to do it, and a student story showing you how they did it.

What to do

A short tip on how to get the most out of college by making connections, making it work for you, and making and difference

Why to do it

The reasoning and evidence behind the tip based on interviews with students and experience along with my research and experience

How to do it

Practical suggestions, advice, and examples of how to put the tip into practice

Student Story

A short story from a student, sharing their experience so that you can see how the tip might work for you and why.

References

1. Melanie Hanson, "College Dropout Rates [2021" Education Data (blog), November 22, 2021, https://educationdata.org/college-dropout-rates

2. "Students with depression twice as likely to drop out of college," Michigan News, July 10, 2009, https://news.umich.edu/students-with-depression-twice-as-likely-to-drop-out-of-college/.

3. Amy L. Hawkins, "Relationship between Undergraduate Student Activity and Academic Performance," Purdue e-Pubs, April 23, 2010, 41.

4. "Implementation intention," *Wikipedia*, June 23, 2021, https://en.wikipedia.org/w/index.php?title=Implementation_intention&oldid=1030077453.

Part 1

Know Yourself and Your College Options

1

Knowing Yourself

To get the most out of college, you have to design your experience. To do this, you need to know who you are designing for: you! This section will help you understand yourself so that you can get the most out of your college experience.

Understanding Yourself

Knowing who you are can take a lifetime, but you can get started now to inform your college search. First, think about why are you going to college in the first place – what might you want to get out of it? Of course, it's hard to have this all figured out up front, and after all, part of what you do in college is explore and find a path, but it helps to have some ideas. Once you do, then you can understand your interests and strengths and think about the kind of career and impact you want to have. Reflect on the relationships you value today, the knowledge you have today, and how these might be either questioned or continued.

Use the Search and Application Process

Thinking about and learning about yourself doesn't have to happen in isolation, though. You can use guides and search tools at your high school. You can use your college search and application process to prompt it. You can dig into college ratings, reviews, and websites to see what clicks (pun intended).

Try Before You Buy

You can find ways to imagine what it will be like to "try before you buy" through sampling college on walks, tours, events, classes, or other programs. You can squeeze every ounce of value from your admissions tour and even think about your applications not as something to dread but another way to learn.

A 2017 Pew Research Study found that there were more than ten million college applications that year,[1] about seven applications per student. This section will help you know yourself before you go to college so your application – and later, your experience – will stand out.

3

Tip 1. Think about why you are going to college.

Understanding why you are going to college will help you find the right college and get the most out of it. Some students may have family members or friends offering advice and suggestions, or even telling them where to go or what to study. (Who is influencing you?) For some students, going to college is just what is done and they haven't thought much about it. Other students may have specific goals and may be weighing the costs against the benefits. These goals tend to be about discovering who you are and forging your identity, meeting people and building a network, learning about topics of interest, or getting a credential like a degree or certificate that leads to a career.

Research on self-determination theory[2] has uncovered that some people are driven by something inside themselves, while others are motivated more by external rewards and what other people think of them. When people are internally motivated, it's based on their needs to become skilled at something ("competence"), to be connected to a community ("relatedness"), and to have a sense of independence ("autonomy"). Some studies have found that students going to college to fulfill these internal needs are more likely to stay in school and get better grades versus people who are externally driven.[3]

Think about why you are going to college and let that intention inform your choices — and know that it may change as you learn and grow. Have frank and realistic conversations about what it's going to cost, what you can afford, and what it will be worth to you and your family. In the words of one student,

> I didn't know a lot about career paths. Your family pushes you into medicine, engineering, or into the social sector to help your community. It's better to ask, "What are my interests?" then find a mentor whose career relates to them. When you work backwards from careers that are interesting, you can make better choices.

Now's a good time to stop, think, and write it down.

I'm going to college because

_____

_____

_____

Tip 2. Learn, play to, and communicate your strengths.

Understanding what your strengths and interests are will help you decide where to go, what to study, and potential career paths to pursue.

Thus, you need to understand (or remind yourself) what your strengths are and use them in everything from classes to clubs to career.

To understand your strengths, you can take a free assessment, such as the Myers Briggs 16 personalities[4] test or the High5 Test or others,[5] or you can take one you may have to pay for, such as StrengthsFinder[6] (some are free through your school). You can also take an introductory psychology course that features these kinds of assessments. Some of these tests that you may come across online may not be reputable, so ask a guidance counselor, teacher, or mentor if you're not sure.

These assessments will give you information to help you discover your strengths instead of relying on what people have told you to do.

Then you can look for opportunities to play to your strengths, communicate these, and advocate for yourself. Many assessments have practice exercises. Class projects, working with your professors, or on a club activity are also great opportunities to see what it feels like to lean into what you're good at. If it doesn't feel great, it's also okay to explore something else.

> ▌▌ *Something I didn't understand going into my education was that for undergraduate students, the process of learning is a process of discovery. There's so much that you don't know about yourself and the world. I was pressed to have an idea of what my goal was. The best way to do that is to get involved outside of classes.* ▌▌

Tip 3. Think about the most important relationships you have with your family and friends today.

What do you value in these relationships – is it love, support, challenge, inspiration, ideas, community, belief in you, and/or something else?

Let those values inform your college search and your journey through college so you can find these relationships in college. Tom Ellett, a student experience expert and one of the first customer experience officers (CXOs) in higher education,[7] recommends that students reflect in two important ways:

- *To inform your search*, look for a college where people talk informally – not just on the college website – about the relationships among students, faculty, and staff. Look for this in ratings and review sites. Look for descriptions of the campus culture and climate.

- *To inform your college journey*, look for opportunities to create the relationships you value among your friends and with your professors or high school teachers. Think about the people you interact with in your classes and clubs, be intentional about the love, support, challenge, inspiration, ideas, community, and other things you value.

Reflecting on your current relationships will also help you as you think about who to turn to for advice on applications or who to ask for a letter of recommendation. You will also realize that as you look for a college, you aren't just the interviewee, you are also the interviewer – you can ask about the culture, the resources, and the atmosphere of the colleges you consider.

Tip 4. Think about how you know what you know— and what you're ready to question.

Entering college is a good time to think about how you've come to believe what you do, know what you do, and think how you do.

Student experience expert Tom Ellett recommended that students ask themselves: How much of your "cup" has been filled by your parents, teachers, coaches, or other influential adults in your life? How much of your life or career plans are what someone told you to do or to be? Similarly, belonging expert and Virginia Union University Provost Dr. Terrell Strayhorn recommended students ask themselves: How did you come to believe what you do?

With this in mind, you can start the process – which can take much of your adult life! – to rethink what you think, know, and believe, and then answer these questions for yourself. This process of unlearning and unbelieving – asking questions about yourself and your work – is how you learn and grow.

To do this, try to find a community and culture where this kind of questioning and critical thinking are championed. Seek out relationships with people who are different from you in terms of lived experience, race, age, ability, religion, sexual orientation, and other characteristics.

> ❚❚ *It was a shock for me. I wasn't aware of my race and ethnicity until I came to the states. You become more aware of who you are and what race plays in your identity. Then you learn all the different places people come from, all the different backgrounds. Everyone has a different path, different ancestry. It was encouraging to meet people from different places and cultures in just one classroom with thirty people.* ❚❚

Tip 5. Get on college websites and keep clicking.

Ratings and review sites are great resources. A college's website also has great information, but it's probably buried pretty deep. When I talked to the college counseling experts at IvyWise,[8] they suggested that students go online and keep clicking (and clicking) to find these treasures:

- *Want to get a feel for what you might study?* Go to the "Academics" section to explore majors, minors, certificates, concentrations, and however else they organize classes into areas of focus. Look for special programs like summer enrichment/jumpstart, the first-year experience, or study abroad.

- *Want to get a sense of how you might get involved?* Go to the "Student Life" or "Campus Life" or "Student Experience" section to get a sense of the clubs, community, and social climate. What activities that you are doing now will you be able to continue? What new things can you explore?

- *Want to see if the social life suits you?* Go to the social media feeds to get a sense of what's happening at the college. What does the voice, tone, and climate feel like? What are students doing and saying? (You'll want to check out the official channels as well as students' own "unfiltered" feeds on YouTube, Instagram, TikTok, Snapchat, and more.)

When you do this for a bunch of colleges, you'll be able to see how they are different and what feels like a better fit for you as you narrow your list to apply to four to eight of them. Do you get a different sense from your "reach schools" versus "match schools" versus "safety schools"? Don't be afraid to use other sources and sites too.

▐▐Sometimes websites are hard to navigate. Sometimes it takes a long time for the college to respond if you ask them something. I went to Reddit to get faster responses. It's a big community, but you can't always trust Reddit either. ▐▐

Tip 6. Find ways to "sample" going to college.

There are lots of low-stakes ways to learn about colleges. Do this early so you're more informed and comfortable. Later, it becomes more stressful, you have less time, and it costs more. Even before it's time for a tour or overnight visit to a college you are interested in, you can sample a nearby campus (or travel to see one). Some of the ways to do that include the following:

- Stopping by and just walking around with no agenda to see what's happening and how it feels.

- Checking out a few college social media channels on YouTube, Instagram, Snapchat, and more – both the official ones and students' own feeds where you'll get things unfiltered.

- Attending free events or workshops that a local college is offering – they have a surprising number of community programs that you can find on their events calendar.

- Taking a class for credit if you are eligible, as this will give you a sense of what classes are like and what the rhythm of college is.

- Going to the alumni center and asking to talk to alums (most schools have "ambassador" programs) about their experience.

- Attending a summer jumpstart or enrichment program after your senior year that can ease the transition to college, build your skills, and refresh your memory.

- Participating in a summer study program where you spend a couple weeks or more living in the dorms and taking classes, exploring an interest or major as well as the campus. Many of these programs offer scholarships.

While you are sampling college like this, look for colleges that *show* you experience rather than just *tell* you about it. See what students there do and what their experience is like.

Taking some community college classes made the transition much easier. I felt awkward. I was so young. But it helped a lot. I learned what a syllabus is, how and when classes meet. I worked on some of my weaknesses. I was more ready for college.

Tip 7. Get the most from your admissions tour.

Real and virtual tours are a great way to learn about the schools you are interested in. If you are taking the time to do these – especially if you are traveling for them – you want to squeeze every bit of value out of them.

Try to see yourself on the campus by visiting the places you might take classes and study in and by going to the centers for different groups you identify with in terms of interests, race, sexual orientation, veteran status, and more. Talk to real students at these centers in the process. Do the same online by checking out official and students' own social media feeds on YouTube, Instagram, TikTok, Snapchat, and more. Along the way, be sure to take notes (in a specific notebook or in an app) because you may have back-to-back visits and details can get blurred.

> ▌▌ *The tour does a lot to make the college seem inviting. But asking some tough questions is key. Spend some extra time. Have a look around. Eat in the dining hall. Speak to more students and faculty.* ▌▌

Look beyond the buildings to find the people who are there to help you. It's easy to think of a college as a president and professors, but there's a ton of staff there to help you (about 2,500,000 in the US alone![9]) who you should talk to; for example, admission counselors, academic advisors, financial aid officers, or administrators in a department/school you might major in.

When in doubt, ask the admissions office and tour guides. They can point you in the right direction as to who to talk to, where to go, and what to research to answer your questions.

> ▌▌ *Tour guides are students who have been through what you are about to endure as a freshman in college. They can be great resources too, and they're there because they enjoy the campus, want others to come, and are easy to talk to.* ▌▌

And remember, look for opportunities to be shown – not just told about – the college. Seeing is believing.

Tip 8. Use the application process to learn about yourself.

You can dread your college applications, or you can use them to help you learn about yourself and imagine yourself in college. This will not only help you choose and get in, but what you learn will help you design a better experience once you're there.

As Jeff Selingo, author of *Who Gets In and Why* observed, "The best college searches are those that help applicants discover themselves on their way to becoming adults."[10]

When I interviewed the college admissions counseling experts at IvyWise, they suggest you ask yourself three key questions to learn about yourself and imagine yourself in college:

- *Reflect on today:* What activities you are doing now and what you want to continue. Imagine yourself in college. Are you still playing the same sport? Still on the debate team? Playing the same instrument?

- *Ask about tomorrow:* Take some pressure off by not asking yourself "Who do I want to be?" at first. Instead, ask yourself, "What do I want to explore?" Maybe it's something you've been curious about, like learning a language.

- *Think about what's unique:* What makes you unique and what you can contribute. Most applications will ask you what perspective you will bring and how you'll contribute to the community.

Reflection Activity: Knowing Yourself

To make the most of this section, you need to reflect on what you've read, commit to some tips to try, and plan to apply them by thinking about what you'll do if you get stuck or have a problem – what's called an "if-then plan."

From the chapter you just read, what might you want to try?

- Think about why you are going to college.
- Learn, utilize, and communicate your strengths.
- Reflect on your current relationships and what they tell you about the future.
- Think about how you know what you know – and what you're ready to question.
- Get on college websites and keep clicking.
- Find ways to "sample" going to college.
- Get the most from your admissions tour.
- Use the application process to learn about yourself.

IF: **What might be challenging about using these tips?**

_____

_____

_____

_____

THEN: **What will you do to overcome these challenges?**

_____

_____

_____

_____

START: **What's one thing you can do right now?**

_____

_____

References

1. Drew Desilver, "A Majority of U.S. Colleges Admit Most Students Who Apply," Pew Research Center (blog), April 9, 2019, https://www.pewresearch.org/fact-tank/2019/04/09/a-majority-of-u-s-colleges-admit-most-students-who-apply/.

2. "Theory," Center for Self-Determination Theory, accessed September 29, 2021, https://selfdeterminationtheory.org/theory/.

3. Douglas A. Guiffrida et al., "Do Reasons for Attending College Affect Academic Outcomes? A Test of a Motivational Model from a Self-Determination Theory Perspective," *Journal of College Student Development 54, no. 2* (2013): 121–39, https://doi.org/10.1353/csd.2013.0019.

4. "Free Personality Test," 16 Personalities, accessed September 29, 2021, https://www.16personalities.com/.

5. Nicole Celestine, "9 Strength Finding Tests and Assessments You Can Do Today," PositivePsychology.com, June 7, 2019, https://positivepsychology.com/strength-finding-tests/.

6. "StrengthsFinder 2.0," Gallup, Inc., accessed September 29, 2021, https://www.gallup.com/cliftonstrengths/en/254033/strengthsfinder.aspx.

7. Tom Ellett, "Masked and Engaged," Inside Higher Ed., accessed September 30, 2021 https://www.insidehighered.com/views/2021/03/30/building-campus-culture-and-enhancing-student-experience-during-covid-19

8. "College Admissions Counseling," IvyWise, accessed September 29, 2021, https://www.ivywise.com/.

9. National Center for Education Statistics, IPEDS Trend Generator, "Number of people employed by postsecondary institutions," excluding "Instructional" occupational category, accessed September 30, 2021.

10. Jeff Selingo, *Who Gets In and Why: A Year Inside College Admissions* (New York: Scribner, 2020), 55.

2

Knowing Your College Options

As of 2020, there were about 4,000 degree-granting colleges and universities in the US,[1] according to the National Center for Education Statistics. That's a lot of colleges to learn about and choose from – and it's worth noting that for a variety of reasons, some students don't have a lot of options when it comes to college; for example, you may need to study close to home. That's okay too.

Start with Who You Are

Designing your college experience starts before you get there. I get it – it can feel like a lot of pressure to make the right choice. Start with who you are today and what you want to explore in the future. Combine this with an understanding of how colleges and universities work, what makes some stand out, and how to get beyond the rankings, reviews, and ratings.

Know Your Choices

Putting these together to find the right fit is important because many students face an uphill battle to thrive in college despite good intentions, great focus, and lots of hard work. But if you know what to look for, you can tip the scales in your favor to get the most out of college. Remember there are multiple paths into and through college. If it can't happen now, maybe it can later. If you can only take one class to start, that's a great start.

Keep an Open Mind

Maybe the best thing you can do is keep an open mind. Don't narrow down your list of options too quickly to what's nearby, what you assume you can afford, or the most recognizable brands because you've heard their names on ESPN or they are in the Ivy League.

Keep It Organized

It can be confusing to keep all this straight. One thing to consider is creating a table so you can compare the different colleges are you thinking about. Make each horizontal row a thing you care about (like setting, size, and specialization) and make each vertical a column a school. Take notes as you go online, talk to someone, or visit a campus and do this in a specific notebook or in an app. Then, use this to fill in your table.

This section has a few key things to look for: a college that's focused on you, that sees academics and student life as complementary rather than divided, that brings together different support services so they are easier for you to access, that's the right size and setting for you, and where you'll be able to find your voice and use it to make a difference.

Be sure to check out Part 3, in which each chapter covers the needs of a specific student identity, how colleges can support each these types of students, and what to look for in a college.

Tip 9. Choose a college that's the best size and setting for you.

In choosing a college, you want access to people who are present and accessible, who get you and speak your language, and who offer opportunities that align with your skills and interests. There are many sizes, types, and settings of colleges, so you should consider the following:

Setting. Urban colleges are knit into and identify with the cities they are in, whereas suburban campuses have a clearer identity of their own. Are you looking for something similar to or different than what you are used to in terms of people and environment? What's more important to you: great restaurants across the street or a quad to play frisbee on? College towns can offer a bit of both.

Distance. How close or far it is from home is also a factor to consider. Do you want to be able to come home for dinner easily? Come home for the weekend with a little planning? Will it be okay to need an airline ticket to get home?

Size. Larger colleges can provide more opportunities (clubs, sports, classes, and more), but smaller colleges can provide a more intimate community. What's more important to you: every student organization you can imagine or super easy access to your professors in and out of the classroom? Sometimes a small department or school with a strong sense of community at a large university offers the best of both.

Research. The amount and importance of research – creating new knowledge – happening at a college or university influences what kind of place it is. More research means more graduate students. It may mean less focus on teaching as research projects compete for professors' time. However, more research also creates opportunities for students to work on inspiring projects, apply what they are learning, and connect with industry.

Specialization. Somewhat related to size is how broad or specialized a school is. For instance, it might be focused on the arts or aerospace. It might be single sex. It might have a religious affiliation. It might focus on serving primarily students of a certain race such as an HBCU (Historically Black College and University) or HSI (Hispanic-serving institution). Or it might be broad and not have any of these specializations.

Tip 10. Go to a college that's student centered.

College and universities are complicated places whose structures, systems, processes, and policies are often not designed with you in mind. They are "the way we've always done it," even though a lot has changed.

Student-centered colleges do the opposite. They configure their programs, people, processes, and places around today's students. As Paul Quinn College President Michael Sorrell says,

❚❚ *we have to stop being more in love with our traditions than we are with our students.* **❚❚**

When choosing a college, look for one that's focused on putting students first. Some signs of this might be

- They mention "student experience" or "student success" as a goal in their strategic plan (which is typically found in the "About Us" page online).

- They use student-centered language; for instance, they say "student financial services" instead of "bursar."

- They have student-centered processes and policies; for instance, offices that have evening hours and don't require paper-based forms that you have to come in to sign or drop off.

- They have student-centered systems like a "one-stop shop" for student services or a student success center.

- They listen to students and incorporate their voices when making decisions about policies and processes that will impact students; for instance, they have student advisory boards set up to give input.

The good news is that colleges and universities are becoming more student centered. They are recognizing that resources and opportunities haven't always been equally available or fairly distributed. They are shifting from just providing students access to ensuring their success by providing the right support.

As student success expert Dr. Terrell Strayhorn from Virginia Union University told me,

❚❚ *Colleges were led to believe that what students do in college matters more than who they are. Now they realize that what you do in college is shaped by who you are.* **❚❚**

Tip 11. Prepare for outdated college policies and processes.

While they are getting better, many colleges and universities are structured in a way that makes them hard for students to navigate. There is a big divide between academics (what colleges call "academic affairs") and student life (what they call "student affairs"). Students can get caught in the middle.

Be prepared to bridge some divides between academic and social life because this will be critical for your success; for instance, find a group of other students to study with or work on class projects with.

While not always a bad thing, one example of a divide within colleges is that the career services office is twice as likely to be part of student affairs than academic affairs.[2] This can make advice about your career too separated from academic advising about what courses to take and how you're progressing.

As Dr. Strayhorn told me,

> For too long, the burden has been on students and families to figure it out, to find a way, to work around the barriers, and to get an extra personal counselor or advisor.

Savvy students figure out how to bridge these divides and find ways to make the systems work for them. Some universities create student service hubs to support the whole student; for instance, a library may also have counseling, career development, and financial aid in it. But students can fall through the cracks or give up after getting the "runaround" from office to office.[3]

To bridge this academic/student life divide, ask questions; for instance, ask a career advisor about which courses will help for an internship. If you're talking to an advisor, don't leave without an answer to your question or without knowing who to see to get an answer. Don't waste your time sticking with your assigned advisor if they aren't helpful, either. Have a frank conversation about their approach to advising, and if you're not satisfied, ask for a new one.

Tip 12. Look for a "one-stop shop."

College and universities that bring their services together tend to be more student focused. If they don't, you may get the runaround[4] from one place (or website) to another. For example, let's say you go online to register for classes, but the system says you can't, so you go to the registrar's office. There, they tell you it's because of a problem with your bill. Then you go to the finance office, where they tell you there's an issue with your financial aid. At the financial aid office, you finally find out it's because there was a typo in your social security number, which delayed your student loan coming through.

This is exactly what you want to avoid. At a one-stop shop, you can get more help with less hassle. This is critical at larger places that are harder to navigate, but many smaller schools end up as one-stop shops by virtue of their size. A Rand report of four community college systems found that providing a one-stop shop was associated with a 3-percentage-point increase in student persistence (students continuing their studies rather than dropping out).[5]

It's usually easy to find out if a college has a one-stop shop by going on their website. Getting financial aid, paying your bill, and registering for classes is the most common administrative one-stop. Student success centers for tutoring, mentoring, coaching, and skills workshops are another common combo to look for.

Going to a one-stop shop is not only useful for getting services and support, it's also a great way to meet people who will help you feel like you belong and give you advice.

❚❚ *Talking to people ahead of you is key. I talked to seniors about what worked for them. I've done a lot of internships too. A lot of it is trial and error. Some things are fun. Some things are not. My interests have changed too.* ❚❚

Tip 13. Find a place where you'll have a voice.

In so many aspects of life, control and satisfaction go hand in hand. In the workplace, having control over where, when, and how you work makes you much more likely to be enthusiastic about and committed to your work.[6]

In college, an important element of control is having a voice and a sense that it matters. In a national student survey on student experience that I created, students consistently rate "having a say" as the aspect of campus culture they are least satisfied with, rating it only 3.2 out of 5.[7]

If part of going to college is about finding your voice, go to a place where you can use it. This means going to a college that listens to students by having student advisory boards and working closely with the student government. It also means going to a college that wants you to be the creator of your college experience; for instance, they encourage students to start clubs and lead projects.

Look for a school where your opinion is asked for and counts. Talk to current students about this and ask about advocacy and activism. Look for surveys of the "campus climate" online. See what student leadership opportunities are available through clubs and student government.

My campus didn't have one, so I started an Ignite chapter for empowering women. I learned to not be afraid to use my voice. Now I'm helping other women use their voice and feel the same way. If you can't find it on your campus, find it on your own and find a way to bring it to campus. There are other people who feel the same way and haven't said anything.

Tip 14. Think about why, how, and when to involve your parents or other family members.

Part of developing your own identity as an independent adult in college is finding the right ways and amounts to involve your parents, guardians, or other family members. Social science researchers identified this as combining secure attachment to your parents with a healthy separation from them.[8] Secure attachment gives you the confidence to explore and experiment. Healthy separation gives you the independence to develop your own identity.

Getting this balance right is important. A 2007 NASPA study using data from the National Survey of Student Engagement (NSSE) found that students who talked with their parents frequently and whose parents contacted the college on their behalf participated in more college activities and were more satisfied but also reported significantly lower grades.[9]

Set boundaries with your family so you have shared expectations about how much they'll be involved. There are also good ways to check how you are doing, such as the Psychological Separation Inventory (PSI), which measures your functional, emotional, conflictual, and attitudinal independence from your parent(s) or guardian(s).[10]

> *Sitting down and having a conversation about expectations and communications levels was important, especially in my first semester. My mom would get worried if I didn't text her back right away and would text my roommate. We had to talk specifically about when I could respond. I had to help her let go.*

Tip 15. Look for a college that offers value.

All the tips in this book help get the most out of college. This may be easier or harder at some schools, and so you can look for one that offers value to get even more.

There are different ways to think about value, which will relate to why you may be going to college in the first place, reasons like discovering who you are and forging your identity, meeting people and building a network, learning about topics of interest, or getting a credential such as a degree or certificate that leads to a career.

One important way to think about this is financially: as a college graduate, will you earn more than you would have if you didn't go? Will that increase pay for what you spent on tuition and fees? This is simple return on investment or ROI calculation. In general, education pays off, as researchers at Georgetown University have found,[11] but it depends on the choice you make, and it's also a function of what the school offers.

- There are more and more tools to understand the ROI of college. A simple one is the US Department of Education's College Scorecard[12] which shows the cost, graduation rate, and salary after graduation — by major or "field of study." The newly released Equitable Value Explorer is another useful tool to look up how specific colleges provide a return on investment for tuition compared to salaries.[13] The website Payscale also compares cost data and salary data in its ROI tool.[14] You can influence the variables in the ROI equation: where you go based on what it costs and what you study based on what your future salary is likely to be.

- The other aspect of value is qualitative: what does the college offer based on your investment of time and money? Will your professors be accessible and focused on teaching? Will housing be organized to build a sense of community and belonging? Will there be opportunities for you to become a leader and get the training to do so? Will there be opportunities for you to apply what you are learning in the classroom on a project or internship? Will they help you find and develop along a career path? Do they offer ways to accelerate, such as graduating in three years?

Tip 16. Look for scholarship opportunities.

Public, four-year colleges cost more than three times what they were thirty years ago, and private ones cost more than two times what they were.[15] With college becoming more and more expensive, it's increasingly important to look for different kinds of financial aid and scholarships.

First, even if you may not want it or need it, fill out the FAFSA[16] (Free Application for Federal Student Aid), since this is what schools use to evaluate your need.

It takes time to get all the info together. You'll need personal info, such as your social security number – and alien registration number if not a US citizen – and you'll need financial information, such as tax returns and bank statements. If you are financially dependent on your parents/guardians, you'll need this info for them too. Don't be shy about asking questions if you get stuck completing it.

❚❚ Even if you don't think you are going to apply for financial aid, do the FAFSA. There's so much money out there, in scholarships too. You have to apply even if you don't think you'll get it. You might get a thousand dollars, which is a thousand dollars you don't have to pay yourself. ❚❚

Second, look for and apply for scholarships[17] through your school and outside of it. Start by looking at sites like scholarships.com, fastweb.com, chegg.com, niche.com, and collegeboard.org. Beyond the national scholarships that may be national, look locally too, as these may be less competitive. There may be an application, essay, or letters of recommendation needed – many of this can be reused from application to application. Keep in mind that if your state doesn't offer your major, they may have an arrangement where you can go to another state school to take it and only pay the in-state rate for it. If you're on the fence about applying for something, go ahead and do it.

❚❚ Apply for everything. People are afraid to apply to things because they think that a lot of other students are applying, but they aren't. ❚❚

Tip 17. Don't borrow too much money for college.

As of February of 2021, forty-five million current and former students collectively owe $1.7 trillion in student loan debt.[18] About 40 percent of the reason students drop out before graduation is financial.[19] More than 85 percent of students say their loans are a "major source of stress."[20]

"Too much" is a relative term, depending on what college costs and how easy or hard it will be for you to pay for it. To avoid borrowing too much for college, think about these two aspects and what you can do to control them. Think in terms of value: what it costs versus what you get and what it will pay off – See Tip 15 for more on this.

- *What it costs.* Look at the tuition, fees, housing, food, and other costs that may apply each year – often called the "cost of attendance" by a college. Think about how long it may take you to get your degree and how this might go; for instance, maybe you'll start at a two-year community college to get an associate's degree and transfer to a four-year school to get a bachelor's degree? Maybe you'll be studying part-time while you work? Will you be living on campus or at home? What can you control to make it more or less affordable?

- *How you'll pay for it.* Start by completing the application for financial aid (see Tip 16), look for scholarships and grants that reduce loan amounts (also in Tip 16), and look for a campus job – especially one that reinforces or complements what you are studying (see tip 38). Look for the lowest interest rate and whether or not interest is added while you're in school ("unsubsidized") or if the government pays this interest while you're there ("subsidized"). Look at the salary after graduation on sites like College Scorecard[21] or Payscale[22] to be sure that what you might study will enable you to pay off what you do borrow for college.

Reflection Activity: Knowing Your Options

To make the most of this section, you need to reflect on what you've read, commit to some tips to try, and plan to apply them by thinking about what you'll do if you get stuck or have a problem – what's called an "if-then plan."

From what you just read, what might you want to try?

- Go to a college that's the best size and setting for you.
- Go to a college that's student centered.
- Prepare for outdated college structures.
- Look for a "one-stop shop."
- Find a place where you'll have a voice.
- Find the right amount to involve your parents or other family members.
- Look for a college that offers value.
- Look for scholarship opportunities.
- Don't borrow too much money for college.

IF: **What might be challenging about using these tips?**

_____

_____

_____

_____

THEN: **What will you do to overcome these challenges?**

_____

_____

_____

_____

START: **What's one thing you can do right now?**

_____

_____

References

1. National Center for Education Statistics, "Digest of Education Statistics, 2020," accessed September 29, 2021, https://nces.ed.gov/programs/digest/d20/tables/dt20_317.10. asp?current=yes.

2. National Association of Colleges and Employers, "Trends Continue for Career Services' Location, Reporting Structure," October 4, 2019, https://www.naceweb.org/career-development/trends-and-predictions/trends-continue-for-career-services-location-reporting-structure/.

3. Elliot Felix and Adam Griff, "Ending the Runaround: 12 Steps to Integrated Student Services," *brightspot strategy* (blog), May 15, 2019, https://www.brightspotstrategy.com/integrated-student-services-best-practices/.

4. Ibid.

5. Lindsay Daugherty, William R. Johnston, and Tiffany Berglund, "Connecting College Students to Alternative Sources of Support: The Single Stop Community College Initiative and Postsecondary Outcomes," RAND Corporation, April 29, 2020, https://www.rand.org/pubs/research_reports/RR1740-1.html.

6. Steelcase Inc, "Steelcase Report: 5 Key Findings around Employee Engagement," accessed September 29, 2021, https://info.steelcase.com/global-employee-engagement-workplace-comparison.

7. "Student Journey Mapping," brightspot strategy, accessed September 29, 2021, https://www.brightspotstrategy.com/our-services/service-student-experience-snapshot/.

8. Suzanne Bartle-Haring, Penny Brucker, and Ellen Hock, "The Impact of Parental Separation Anxiety on Identity Development in Late Adolescence and Early Adulthood," *Journal of Adolescent Research* 17 (September 2002): 439–50, https://doi.org/10.1177/0743558402175001.

9. Linda J. Sax and Katherine Lynk Wartman, "Studying the Impact of Parental Involvement on College Student Development: A Review and Agenda for Research," in Higher Education: Handbook of Theory and Research, ed. John C. Smart, vol. 25, Higher Education: Handbook of Theory and Research (Dordrecht: Springer Netherlands, 2010), 219–55, https://link.springer.com/chapter/10.1007%2F978-90-481-8598-6_6

10. Daniel Lapsey, Kenneth Rice, Gregory Shadid, "Psychological Separation and Adjustment to College," *Journal of Counseling Psychology* 36, no. 3 (1989): 286–94, https://psycnet.apa.org/buy/1989-38171-001.

11. "Ranking ROI of 4,500 US Colleges and Universities," Georgetown University Center on Education and the Workforce, accessed September 30, 2021. https://cew.georgetown.edu/cew-reports/collegeroi/

12. "College Scorecard," US Department of Education, accessed September 30, 2021. https://collegescorecard.ed.gov/

13. "Equitable Value Explorer," accessed November 30, 2021. https://www.postsecondaryvalue.org/equitable-value-explorer/

14. "Best Value Colleges," Payscale, accessed September 30, 2021. https://www.payscale.com/college-roi

15. "Trends in College Pricing," College Board, accessed September 30, 2021. https://research.collegeboard.org/trends/college-pricing.

16. "FAFSA® Application," accessed September 29, 2021, https://studentaid.gov/h/apply-for-aid/fafsa.

17. Farran Powell and Emma Kerr, "How to Find and Secure Scholarships for College," US News & World Report, February 5, 2020, https://www.usnews.com/education/best-colleges/paying-for-college/articles/how-to-find-and-secure-scholarships-for-college.

18. Zack Friedman, "Student Loan Debt Statistics In 2021: A Record $1.7 Trillion," Forbes, February 20, 2021, https://www.forbes.com/sites/zackfriedman/2021/02/20/student-loan-debt-statistics-in-2021-a-record-17-trillion/

19. Melanie Hanson, "College Dropout Rates [2021" Education Data (blog), November 22, 2021, https://educationdata.org/college-dropout-rates

20. Diana Hembree, "New Report Finds Student Debt Burden Has 'Disastrous Domino Effect' on Millions of Americans," Forbes, November 1, 2018, https://www.forbes.com/sites/dianahembree/2018/11/01/new-report-finds-student-debt-burden-has-disastrous-domino-effect-on-millions-of-americans.

21. "College Scorecard," US Department of Education, accessed September 30, 2021. https://collegescorecard.ed.gov/.

22. "Best Value Colleges," Payscale, accessed September 30, 2021. https://www.payscale.com/college-roi.

Part 2

General Advice to Set Your Foundation

3

Thriving in Class

While they aren't everything, academics are the biggest part of your college experience. I designed a national survey[1] that asked college students how they'd allocate their tuition across all the different aspects of college. Students placed about half the value in classes and research projects, about a quarter of the value in student services and community, and the remaining quarter in access to technology and the campus.

Making the most of your college experience means getting the most from academics. To do this you need to make connections and go beyond the classrooms.

Make Connections so that 1+1=3

Making connections means adopting a "connector" mindset so that everything you do connects different aspects of your life; for instance, attend an event, then write about it for your journalism class (or the school paper), or find a way for the same project to fulfill the requirements for two classes. Use your campus job to also make friends or try out a career path.

Go Beyond the Classroom

Going beyond the classroom means more than showing up for class, taking the tests, and turning in the paper. Use your class projects as ways to explore career paths by interviewing someone (which might come in handy when it's time for an internship) or working with a real organization like a nonprofit nearby so you can build your confidence and your resume while making an impact. Going to your professors' "office hours" – whether to say hi, get advice, or ask a question about class – is also a great way to go beyond the classroom. Working with them on their research is too.

No matter what you do, it will be hard. And that's okay. That doesn't mean you don't belong. It probably just means it's worth doing and you're growing. The most rewarding and meaningful things in life are often the hardest.

Tip 18. Set task-based goals to motivate yourself.

Setting goals gives you something concrete to strive for and hold yourself accountable to. It's what behavioral scientists refer to as a "commitment device" – you are more likely to do something once you explicitly commit to doing it, especially when you do so publicly.

In addition to "soft" commitment devices, such as setting goals, there are "hard" commitment devices, which force you to comply, like a savings account you can't withdraw from or software like Offtime[2] or Moment[3] that blocks social media and other distractions.

A study by economists at MIT of more than 4,000 students found that task-based goals work, but performance-based goals don't. In fact, setting task-based goals worked as well as giving students a $1,000 incentive. It's better to say "I will take ten practice tests" (a task-based goal) rather than "I will get a B+ in calculus" (a performance-based goal).[4]

(The researchers note that setting task-based goals was much more effective for male students, perhaps because of a tendency to be more present biased than female students, who tend to be more future focused).

A good checklist for creating task-based goals is to make them "SMART": specific, measurable, achievable, relevant, and time bound.[5]

Tip 19. Start with courses that build your confidence and help you adjust.

College will be an adjustment. You're in a new place, with new people and new responsibilities. This means that just getting to class on time and doing the work can be a challenge. Try to choose the right courses at the right time. To do this, consider the difficulty of the course, how it fits with a major, and the type of course. You may also want to take a short online quiz in the subject to get a sense of your confidence to start with.

- *Course difficulty:* It's best not to start with very challenging courses your first semester because this makes the adjustment harder and shakes your confidence.

- *Course major:* Many majors have "gateway" courses that lots of future classes build on. Unfortunately, many of these function as "gatekeeper" courses that lots of students withdraw from or fail. Talk to your advisor to identify what the gateway courses are and ask your professors explicitly what you need to do to succeed. Then be proactive about getting help like tutoring (see Tip 32 for more on this) and joining a study group (see Tip 23 for more on this).

- *Course type:* Some studies have also shown that you are better off taking a class focused on methods (like how to do something, such as statistics or design thinking) before you take courses focused on a topic (such as one on climate change).[6] Other studies have found that taking shorter, compressed courses to start with can also help.[7]

- *Course tactics:* Look for courses that are actively working to increase inclusion and student success by applying research. For instance, this study had ESL students read stories that showed how not feeling a sense of belonging was common and temporary, and they completed more credits and got higher grades compared with students who didn't read them.[8]

Of course, who is teaching and how big the class is are important considerations too. Ask around and do your research about the instructor and see if you can take some smaller classes (less than thirty students), where it will be easier to make a connection with your professor.

Tip 20. Interact with other students, in and out of the classroom.

Talking to and working with other students in discussions and projects means you are actively engaging in your learning rather than passively absorbing information.

A study in the *Proceedings of the National Academy of Sciences* found that active learning cut failure rates nearly in half in science, engineering, and math courses. Instead of 34 percent of students failing these courses, 22 percent did when active learning strategies were used.[9]

Active learning could include discussing a topic with the student next to you, working on a project together, participating in class discussions in person and online, or all of these.

It extends beyond the classroom as well when you have meals with different students, volunteer, get involved in intramural sports, join affinity groups, and more. While these may seem separate from your classes, they overlap — a teammate may become your favorite person to study with. All these activities can work together too.

> *I work at a makerspace, am active in the Muslim student association, and go to speaker events where I can hear from people in industry and alumni. By interacting with such a diverse group of people, it helped me learn how to apply things and how things fit together.*

Tip 21. Tell stories with data.

Learning to speak with numbers will serve you well. Data will power the economy even more in the future. There are more and more data and there are more and more ways to gather it, analyze, and visualize it. So it's a good idea to get comfortable expressing your ideas with numbers.

A 2019 survey of more than three hundred companies found that 89 percent said it was a priority for their employees to be fluent with data,[10] and the number of job postings mentioning data analysis jumped 50 percent from 2017 to 2019.[11] As you get increasingly comfortable with data, you'll progress from literacy to fluency. The University of Michigan has a great free book on this.[12]

You can start by understanding basic statistics, for example, what an average is. Then you can progress to finding patterns and creating insights from numbers such as being able to interpret a graph and then create one. Then move to telling stories with data, using evidence to make a compelling case for your idea.

A statistics course is a must. You can add to that with an introductory data science course where you'll apply computing to data – in other words, write code to analyze and visualize data.

A Freakonomics Podcast[13] offers a nice way to start with something simple to demystify all this: go out and collect data on two variables and plot each of the points on a graph – first for two things you think are related, such as the height and shoe size of ten friends, and a second time for two things that probably aren't, such as the sizes and colors of those same shoes. You'll probably see that the first set of points line up, but they are all over the place in the second one.

Tip 22. Use design thinking to identify and solve problems.

Our world is getting more complex, uncertain,[14] and diverse, and it has pressing challenges that are "wicked problems,"[15] such as climate change and income inequality. Many studies have pointed to building the skills that employers look for: creativity, critical thinking, collaboration, communication, and computation (see Tip 69 for more on this).

Design thinking is a mindset and set of skills and tools for creative problem solving which will serve you well in college and in your career. At its core, you'll learn empathy for other people so you can solve problems with them in mind. You'll learn to make things and try things out; you'll learn by experimenting and "prototyping." You'll learn storytelling to communicate your understanding of people and your ideas in compelling ways.

The benefits of design thinking are numerous. One study found students got better at asking for critical thinking and organizing their ideas.[16] Another study found that design thinking can create more inclusive learning environments.[17] Another found it can help students learn from their mistakes.[18]

> ▟▟ Applying design thinking strategies has helped me look beyond my personal experience. By considering how problems affect people with different backgrounds and needs, my solutions have become more inclusive and well rounded. Even if you don't have someone particular in mind, imagining scenarios and different personas will broaden your perspective on the design. ▟▟

Tip 23. Study in groups, especially when the subject matter is hard.

When you study alone and encounter difficult material, you may not realize that it's not you — it's hard for everyone. This can lead to a downward spiral of "imposter syndrome,"[19] failing a course, changing majors, or even dropping out.

For example, in a landmark study at UC Berkeley in the 1980s, Uri Treisman uncovered that studying alone was leading Black students to fail calculus at higher rates (than white students) despite their talent, past success, and hard work.[20]

> *I had a small major so it was easy to form study groups, and you can do homework together on multiple classes. Even if you aren't doing it together, it's so helpful to have someone to talk it out with. Don't feel like you are not allowed to ask questions. Use your resources — your classmates are resources.*

To study in groups, ask your professor or the teaching assistant if they will be organizing groups; if not, organize your own. Aim for three to five people so it's small enough to get together conveniently and create a safe space to help each other. Check out Tip 24 about organizing successful group work too. Study groups may also happen naturally if you're in a living/learning community (See Tip 42) and/or if you are taking multiple classes with the same students.

> *Group chats are really helpful for group work. We all click on the group.me link the first day. It's helpful to see what other students are doing. What they are asking. Seeing things differently helps you understand if you are missing something.*

Tip 24. Organize your group work.

While individual effort will always be an important part of your education, colleges are moving to a more collective approach to learning and research. This approach exposes people to diverse perspectives, helps solve complex problems, and gives students a taste of working in teams or groups, as they will do on the job.

Working in a group on a class project or club event can be awesome or awful. The key to successful group work is to organize the people and the process together.

Start by taking the time to do introductions and learn about your teammates. Then talk about what you are trying to accomplish and write out the goals. Then you can define the roles that you'll each play to achieve them. You need people to lead the group, coordinate the work, energize the group, come up with ideas, evaluate them, and take notes.

With goals and roles established, think about how you'll get things done. Answer the questions: Who will do what by when? How will you meet and communicate? What tools or technology will you use to work? Where and how will you store and organize information? Set some ground rules about being helpful, fair, and understanding.

Finally, think ahead about what the challenges might be. The most common are communication issues, uneven participation, not feeling included, and managing cultural differences. Harvard's Center for Teaching and Learning has some great resources and tips on effective group work, even for things like resolving conflicts.[21]

I found that stating what each person is doing at the start is really important to make sure there aren't any hiccups at the end. We set up deadlines and milestones and stay in touch throughout with group chats on group.me and create a shared doc or folder so everyone can double-check the work.

Tip 25. Connect the dots with your class projects.

You will be asked to do a variety of projects. Rather than get pulled in different directions, try to focus on a topic that fulfills the requirements of multiple classes and connects to something you care about. For instance, maybe you're a climate activist at heart, so your project touches on the Clean Water Act for a political science class and on water quality for an environmental science class?

Connecting the dots like this will not only save you a ton of time. It will also enable you to go into greater depth and start uncovering what you are passionate about so you can learn, build skills, and make an immediate impact. These might include research projects using primary sources or creating presentations, performances, plans, and prototypes. Connecting the dots also helps you reflect on and summarize what you are learning so you can make these connections. Doing this as you go (instead of waiting till the end of the semester or right before the test) is so valuable.

Look for courses that help your local community. This is really good if you are time crunched because then are you able to combine helping your community with your class. As part of my first-year seminar, we worked in a soup kitchen.

This means you'll be working on what are called "renewable assignments" that have an impact in the world. These are rewarding things that contribute to the world that you'll keep coming back to in your spare time because you're passionate about them, versus "disposable assignments" that you forget about the moment you turn them in.[22]

You have certain assignments for a class that you're never gonna touch again. So, being able to connect one subject to another can help. Connect them to something you care about. My course on forestry helped with my projects in architecture. It gave me a different insight I didn't expect. Sometimes this comes down to picking your classes so they go together.

Tip 26. Explore your ideas by making something.

When working on a project, you can make things like drawings, mock-ups, or models that *represent* an idea you already have in your head, or you can make something that helps you *explore* the idea and take you to new places. (Hands-on activities also often have the added benefit of reducing stress too.)

MIT Emeritus Professor Bill Porter's chapter "Designer's Objects" encourages designers not only to communicate ideas with increasing accuracy and detail over time, but also to make things as part of the process of questioning and understanding.[23]

A good way to explore is to do something you can't control, such as drawing with your eyes closed or drawing something in five seconds. This kind of exploration is a great way to remind yourself to stay curious as you're learning.

Exploring your idea by creating something is also a great way to take the pressure off that can stifle things and make you think it has to be perfect. In a recent interview, songwriter Jeff Tweedy noted that you get the most from the creative process when you expect the least from it.[24]

> *I didn't have any exposure to art or design before coming to college.... Now I see that a maker focus is something that every class can benefit from. Sometimes I would get ambiguous feedback from my professor, like "What if you try folding something?" and that led me to unexpected places. Making something with my hands really made a difference.*

Tip 27. Treat everything as an opportunity to grow.

Psychologist Carol Dweck distinguished between a "fixed mindset" where people think their abilities are set and their limits lead to failure versus a "growth mindset" in which challenges, failure, and feedback are opportunities to grow.[25]

A growth mindset will help you gain confidence and self-esteem while reducing anxiety and depression. It also means things just get more fun because every situation you are in is a chance to learn and feel good about that. Here are few important ways to adopt a growth mindset:

- *What you say:* Add the word yet – then you go from "I can't do that" to "I can't do that yet," which can make all the difference. One student I talked to said, "Every day I tell myself: 'You look good, you feel good, you do good.' It reminds me to take the time to take care of myself. Then I end up having a good day."

- *What you do:* When it's time to do something new, don't overthink it. Remember Jerry Sternin's advice: "It's easier to act your way into thinking differently than think your way into acting differently."[26]

- *How you think:* Don't get discouraged if you don't think this way yet. You should also be skeptical if people are sending you the message you can't do something. Go to a different professor or TA when you encounter that. Spend your time with people who believe in you – and tell you that they do.

> *Classes are going to be tougher. The scores we'll get on exams won't be what we want. So, you have to think about the failure you experience as helping you learn. Talking to my friends who are going through the same struggles helps a lot. I also keep in mind what really matters – your projects are more important for a job than your grades.*

Tip 28. Learn something by teaching it.

The best way to learn something is to teach it, for instance, to a friend or family member. This forces you to understand something, apply it, and communicate it – and it helps someone else in the process.

In one study, researchers examined the role of preparing to teach a concept and actually teaching it. Both helped students understand and retain the concepts.[27] One student I talked to noted: "It keeps you motivated. You see yourself ... you become your mentors."

There are lots of ways to do this: sign up to be a peer mentor or peer tutor, help your classmates on group projects, help your friends informally when studying together, or sign up to be a teaching assistant for a class. If you're shy or like to be on your own, you can even practice this by talking to a stuffed animal, rubber duck, or other object and get the benefits of preparing and explaining.

❚❚ I tell myself: "Be the person you wish you had when you were younger." It's difficult for me sometimes, but I'm creating a path for and helping future generations. ❚❚

Tip 29. Work with your professors on their research.

When you work on a long research project with a professor, it gives you the chance to put what you are learning into practice, learn new skills, build relationships, be part of a team, and earn money, since often research grants help pay for the research team.

Not only is this one of the activities mostly likely to cultivate and demonstrate your commitment and curiosity – what the American Association of Colleges and Universities calls a "high-impact practice"[28] – it's one of UMBC President Freeman Hrabowski's "four pillars of student success."[29] Seeing something you've worked on get published and have an impact on society is also its own reward.

> I wasn't sure what to expect. I thought it'd be just doing some research, but it opened so many doors. I met other faculty and made connections. I gave a lecture. I got insight into what professors do outside of teaching that made me want to become one.

Your school likely has an office/center that coordinates and communicates research opportunities, often with ways to try it out over a break. You can also find these yourself by approaching your professors and asking about their work. Even if they don't have a role for you, ask if they have other ideas and about what skills and experience they are looking for so you can pitch those to someone else.

As you contemplate research opportunities, be sure to ask about the goals and structure of the project, who you'll be working with, what the timeline is, and how much the professor will be involved; if they are stretched too thin, it might not be a good experience for you.

Tip 30. Keep in mind that your professors may feel awkward too.

It's tempting to come to class assuming your professors have it all figured out and have all the confidence in the world. In reality, the first day of class (and many that follow) may be awkward and stressful for them too.

Maybe they are teaching something for the first time or in a new place? Or maybe they are trying to bridge the divide in age and experience between you and them? Maybe they are nervous because, like most professors, they know a lot about their subject but were never taught how to teach it?

Look for ways to go beyond transactional comments like "Will this be on the test?" to make a genuine, personal connection with them. This will make things more comfortable for them, and it will make things better for you, your professors, and your class.

Go early to class, say hello, and stay late. Learn to make small talk with your professors about something you just learned, what you are thinking about, or what you are doing on campus. Invite them to something you are going to or are involved in. It can be as simple as "I really enjoyed your class.... Can you recommend additional reading?"

Professors also typically have office hours when they set aside time to meet with students in their office (or at a library or in a café) to answer questions and give advice on the class or college in general. Going to these is another great way to build a relationship with your professors. It can be just to say hello, and if it's to get help or ask a question, that isn't a bad thing. One professor I talked to mentioned:

> ❚❚ *Just like students, I am always very nervous walking into the classroom to begin a semester.... Coming to the class early and talking about their weekend, what is happening on the campus, and how their room situation is are all good ways to engage the students.... Say hi to me, or ask me what I did this weekend and help make me feel comfortable ... it's a two-way street.* ❚❚

Tip 31. Find a mentor.

A mentor might be a professor, staff member, or another student who can guide and encourage your academic and career exploration and development (and help you connect classes and careers). Mentors not only give you advice and set an example to follow, but talking with them helps you make meaning out of what's happening to you. When they help you do this, mentors also help you "learn how to learn" so that you get in the habit of reflecting on and summarizing what you're doing and relating it to your goals, career path, and more.

According to the Gallup-Purdue Index, students who had a mentor who "encouraged me to pursue my goals and dreams" were 1.9 times more likely to find meaningful, engaging work after college.[30]

> ❚❚ *Connections I made in programs in high school have been really valuable, and we've been able to stay in touch even though he's in L.A. He has experience and is a second pair of eyes that I trust. He's also been a role model for me since a lot is new. Mentors relate to what you've been going through.* ❚❚

Instructors from your classes, a professor whose research you are working on, the faculty advisor to your student organization, or alumni can all make great mentors, especially if you have something in common with them to start with. Your school's alumni office often has a mentoring program to connect students to alums (and internships or jobs), and that's a great place to start. Keep in mind that you'll likely have more than one mentor over your college and professional career.

Start by reflecting on what you want to get out of it, then use that to think about who might be able to help. Next, contact potential mentors to introduce yourself; learn about them and be upfront about the advice you're seeking – don't just ask, "Can I pick your brain?"[31]

Reflection Activity: Thriving in Class

To make the most of this section, you need to reflect on what you've read, commit to some tips to try, and plan to apply them by thinking about what you'll do if you get stuck or have a problem – what's called an "if-then plan."

From what you just read, what might you want to try?

- Set goals to motivate yourself.
- Start with courses that build your confidence and help you adjust.
- Interact with other students in and out of the classroom.
- Tell stories with data.
- Use design thinking to identify and solve problems.
- Study in groups, especially when the subject matter is hard.
- Organize your group work.
- Connect the dots with your class projects.
- Explore your ideas by making something.
- Treat everything as an opportunity to grow.
- Learn something by teaching it.
- Work with your professors on their research.
- Remember that your professors feel awkward too.
- Find a mentor.

IF: **What might be challenging about using these tips?**

_____

_____

_____

_____

_____

_____

THEN: **What will you do to overcome these challenges?**

_____

_____

_____

_____

_____

_____

_____

START: **What's one thing you can do right now?**

_____

_____

_____

_____

References

1. "The Impact of COVID-19 on the University Student Experience," Ideas (blog), February 3, 2021, https://www.wework.com/ideas/research-insights/research-studies/the-impact-of-covid-19-on-the-university-student-experience.

2. "OFFTIME App. Unplug, It's Enough," accessed September 29, 2021, https://offtime.app/index.php.

3. "A New App Called Moment Shows You How Addicted You Are to Your IPhone," TechCrunch (blog), June 27, 2014, https://social.techcrunch.com/2014/06/27/a-new-app-called-moment-shows-you-how-addicted-you-are-to-your-iphone/.

4. Damon Clark et al., "Using Goals to Motivate College Students: Theory and Evidence from Field Experiments," Review of Economics and Statistics 102, no. 4 (October 2020): 648–63, https://doi.org/10.1162/rest_a_00864.

5. "SMART Goals: How to Make Your Goals Achievable," Mind Tools, accessed September 29, 2021, http://www.mindtools.com/pages/article/smart-goals.htm.

6. Laura Betancur et al., "Analytical Assessment of Course Sequencing: The Case of Methodological Courses in Psychology," Journal of Educational Psychology 111, no. 1 (January 2019): 91–103, https://doi.org/10.1037/edu0000269.

7. Benjamin R. Gamboa, "Impact of Course Length on and Subsequent Use as a Predictor of Course Success" (Crafton Hills College Report, RRN 688), November 8, 2013, https://www.craftonhills.edu/~/media/Files/SBCCD/CHC/About%20CHC/Research%20and%20Planning/Research%20Briefs/Academic%20Success%20Studies/Compressed%20Course%20Study.pdf.

8. Jennifer LaCosse et al., "A Social-Belonging Intervention Improves STEM Outcomes for Students Who Speak English as a Second Language," Science Advances 6, no. 40 (October 2020): eabb6543, https://doi.org/10.1126/sciadv.abb6543.

9. Scott Freeman et al., "Active Learning Increases Student Performance in Science, Engineering, and Mathematics," Proceedings of the National Academy of Sciences 111, no. 23 (June 2014): 8410–15, https://doi.org/10.1073/pnas.1319030111.

10. Joyce Chiu, "Why 89% of Companies Are Prioritizing Data Fluency," DataCamp (blog), September 18, 2019, https://www.datacamp.com/community/blog/why-89-percent-of-companies-are-prioritizing-data-fluency.

11. Jeff Selingo and Michael Horn, "What's Going on with the Workforce" Future U (podcast, Ep. 89), October 25, 2021, https://www.futureupodcast.com/episodes/whats-going-on-with-the-workforce/

12. Debbie Abilock et al., Creating Data Literate Students (Ann Arbor, MI: Michigan Publishing, University of Michigan Library, 2017), http://dx.doi.org/10.3998/mpub.9873254.

13. Zack Lapinski, "America's Math Curriculum Doesn't Add Up (People I [Mostly] Admire Ep. 42)," Freakonomics (blog), August 27, 2021, https://freakonomics.com/podcast/pima-math-curriculum/.

14. "Volatility, Uncertainty, Complexity and Ambiguity," Wikipedia, accessed September 30, 2021, https://en.wikipedia.org/wiki/Volatility,_uncertainty,_complexity_and_ambiguity.

15. "Wicked problem," Wikipedia, accessed September 30, 2021, https://en.wikipedia.org/wiki/Wicked_problem.

16. Luke David Conlin et al., "Guardian Angels of Our Better Nature: Finding Evidence of the Benefits of Design Thinking," ASEE Annual Conference & Exposition, June 14, 2015, https://peer.asee.org/guardian-angels-of-our-better-nature-finding-evidence-of-the-benefits-of-design-thinking.

17. Sarah L. Rodriguez et al., "Inclusion & Marginalization: How Perceptions of Design Thinking Pedagogy Influence Computer, Electrical, and Software Engineering Identity," *International Journal of Education in Mathematics, Science, and Technology* 8, no. 4 (2020), https://www. ijemst.org/index.php/ijemst/article/view/952.

18. Jenna Marks, "The Impact of a Brief Design Thinking Intervention on Students' Design Knowledge, Iterative Dispositions, and Attitudes Towards Failure," PhD diss., Columbia University., 2017. 10274661.

19. "Managing Imposter Syndrome: Husky Experience Toolkit: University of Washington," accessed September 29, 2021, https://sas.uaa.uw.edu/husky-experience/know-yourself/managing-imposter-syndrome/.

20. "Philip Uri Treisman," Learning and the Adolescent Mind, accessed September 29, 2021, http://learningandtheadolescentmind.org/people_05.html.

21. "Group Work," Harvard University website, accessed September 29, 2021, https://bokcenter. harvard.edu/group-work.

22. "Hendricks, Christina. "Renewable assignments: Student work adding value to the world." University of British Columbia, October 29th, 2015 https://flexible.learning.ubc.ca/news-events/renewable-assignments-student-work-adding-value-to-the-world/

23. William L. Porter, "Designers' Objects," in *Design Representation*, ed. Gabriela Goldschmidt and William L. Porter (London: Springer, 2004), 63–79, https://doi.org/10.1007/978-1-85233-863-3_3.

24. "Wilco's Jeff Tweedy Wants You to Be Bad at Something. It's for Your Own Good," The Ezra Klein Show, *New York Times*, July 2, 2021, https://www.nytimes.com/2021/07/02/opinion/ezra-klein-podcast-jeff-tweedy.html.

25. Carol Dweck, "The Power of Believing that You Can Improve," TEDxNorrkoping 1418832726, November 2014, https://www.ted.com/talks/carol_dweck_the_power_of_believing_that_you_can_improve.

26. Jerry Sternin, Richard T. Pascale, and Monique Sternin, *The Power of Positive Deviance* (Harvard Business Press, 2010), 38.

27. Logan Fiorella and Richard E. Mayer, "Role of Expectations and Explanations in Learning by Teaching," *Contemporary Educational Psychology* 39, no. 2 (April 1, 2014): 75–85, https://doi. org/10.1016/j.cedpsych.2014.01.001.

28. George D. Kuh, "High-Impact Educational Practices," Association of American Colleges & Universities, June 24, 2014, https://www.aacu.org/node/4084.

29. Freeman Hrabowski, "4 Pillars of College Success in Science," TED2013, 1365434089, February 2013. https://www.ted.com/talks/freeman_hrabowski_4_pillars_of_college_success_in_science.

30. "The Gallup-Purdue Index 2015 Report," Gallup, accessed September 29, 2021, https://www. gallup.com/services/185924/gallup-purdue-index-2015-report.aspx.

31. Anna Goldfarb, "The Right Way to Ask, 'Can I Pick Your Brain?'" New York Times, March 17, 2019, https://www.nytimes.com/2019/03/17/smarter-living/the-right-way-to-ask-can-i-pick-your-brain. html.

4

Feeling Supported

Colleges and universities are full of people who want to help you. They are professors, advisors, counselors, coaches, tutors, mentors, and administrators who are knowledgeable, passionate, and dedicated. They are there for the mission and they are there for you.

When I spoke to Dr. Terrell Strayhorn, an expert in student belonging, he made the important point that

> ▟▟ *all college students need support to be successful – financial, academic, emotional, social or all of these – but it's the amount, quality, and forms of support that vary.... You are not inadequate or broken or delayed because you need help. You will be successful because you got help.* ▟▟

Understanding the Resources Available to You

The main thing you need to understand is that sometimes the history and structure of a college gets in the way of helping you. There is a historical (and unhelpful) divide between academics and everything else. As things change, colleges tend to add a new "office" or "center" to help, like a Center for First-Generation Students or a Veterans' Resource Center or an Office of Transfer Students. But this can be confusing: where do students go first if they are first-generation veteran students who just transferred? It can be even harder if you are part of a minority population such as students of color or LGBTQ+ students.

Asking for help and getting support

Try to be proactive about asking for help, asking questions, and advocating for yourself – I know, easier said than done. The good news is, so many colleges and universities have devoted themselves to "student success," that it is becoming easier for students to know what they need, what help is available, and how to get it. You have permission to ask about what resources are available.

It may be that you need advice on what class to take, want to work with a tutor to prep for your calculus test, need to talk to a psychological counselor, need help analyzing data, or want comments on the paper you're writing. Find the right way to get the support you need by going to a center, calling someone, chatting with someone online, or using your college's AI-driven chatbot.

Tip 32. Ask for help.

Whether it's tutoring, counseling, or career advice, asking for help is essential to getting the most out of your college experience and take advantage of the resources and opportunities your college provides. But it is hard. You may not know what help is available. You may not know you need it. You may not feel comfortable asking for it or even feel entitled to it.[1] But you also may be able to get help remotely if that's more comfortable for you, whether it's a virtual advising session or a telehealth counseling session.

Asking for help doesn't mean you've already failed. It's a sign of strength and self-awareness. To become a pro at asking for and getting help, think awareness, assessment, and advocacy:

- *Awareness.* Learn about the resources that are available even before you need them. Attend orientations, go to "Centers" (like a writing center, first gen center, LGBTQ+ center), or talk to friends, family, or professors.

- *Assessment.* Identify when you need help. It may be as simple as a low grade or someone's suggestion. Or it may take some self-reflection and self-awareness. To gain this, you can talk to a friend, professor, mentor, or advisor. There may even be an assessment such as StrengthsFinder that can help you.

- *Advocacy.* Once you know what's available and when you need it, you still have to get comfortable asking for it. First, know that it's normal to ask for help – "A" students go to the writing center for help on a paper. You can also talk to a friend who's gotten similar help or even go with them the next time they do.

Don't be afraid to ask for help. You are not alone. People care about you.... If you don't ask, they won't know either. It's your first resource, not a last resort. It's okay to tell people if things aren't going well.

Tip 33. Practice advocating for yourself.

There are lots of valid reasons students don't speak up or speak out to advocate for themselves or ask for help. Maybe you are afraid of the reaction you might get or of the retribution that might result?

There is after all a power dynamic at play, with a professor or staff member having influence over your high-stakes stuff, such as your finances, immigration status, career, and life goals.

Look for ways to get comfortable asking for help and advocating for yourself by practicing on small-stakes issues where it won't matter to you if the answer is "no";[2] for example, negotiation expert Chris Voss[3] recommends building this skill by asking for small things in everyday life in situations where the stakes are low, like suggesting a new or unusual place to get a meal or switching seats with someone at the movies. Then, you'll get comfortable not taking "no" for an answer; for instance, when meeting with an advisor, don't leave without specific things to do or people to meet.

Student Success Expert Dr. Terrell Strayhorn from Virginia Union University and the educational consultancy Do Good Work[4] has also created "mad lib" style tools to help students practice asking for help and advocating for themselves. He calls these "Higher Ed Libs,"[5] and they contain sentences with blanks to fill in so you can practice what you'll say and get more comfortable saying it.

> *A lot of students get overwhelmed during finals, especially if you have three tests on the same day. Some professors have strict rules about rescheduling, but many are very understanding if you go to them to see if you can extend the deadline or reschedule the exam. You'll never know if they are willing to help you if you don't ask.*

Tip 34. Work with a student success coach.

Coaches can help you uncover or clarify your goals, connect you to resources and information, and keep you on track by identifying obstacles and ways to get around them – for classes and for all the other aspects of student life.

While not all coaching programs prove successful, a 2013 Stanford University study using a randomized sample found that students working with coaches were more likely to stay enrolled (and that this was a cost-effective strategy for colleges to offer).[6]

I love academic coaching because it helped me regain my confidence in obtaining the course material. Also, it has molded me into a more active learner in and out of the classroom. I love all of the study tools and time management skills I have learned that make it easier to study.[7]

Most colleges have a student success center or an office of student success that can connect you with a coach. Like tutoring, success coaching is something that sounds like it costs money but is typically free. Coaching can also complement tutoring on a subject or class by focusing on skills like planning ahead and time management.

My coach helped me take the study skills that I already had and make them ten times better than they were, which helped me to create a better learning opportunity for myself.[7]

Tip 35. Get a variety of help from the library.

In addition to using your library as a place to study, take advantage of its services to support research, writing, data, communication, media, and more. Students who use library resources and services do better academically and are more likely to graduate.

One study showed that students who used library resources were 1.44 times more likely to graduate than those who didn't.[8] Another found that hours spent studying in the library was a particularly good predictor of whether Black students would continue their studies.[9]

One student I talked to reflected on this, realizing they hadn't taken full advantage of what their library had to offer, and said:

> *I never got the help my tuition was paying for.*

Libraries are full of people dedicated to helping you so you can browse their services online, show up in person, or ask a question online through their chat support. When you do, ask for advice and recommendations about what else they offer. This might include:

- Talking with you about the topic of and the print/online sources for a research project

- Receiving feedback on your writing in terms of style, structure, flow, and more

- Gathering, analyzing, and visualizing data such as what software or graph to use

- Understanding your strengths and weaknesses as a presenter to improve them and tell better stories

- Learning how to record, edit, and share a video, whether it's solo on your webcam or a group in front of a green screen

Tip 36. Go to student health (and not just when you're sick).

Student Health Centers have expanded their spaces and offerings in recent years to serve as one-stop-shops for health and wellness, not only when you're sick but for a range of services like nutrition, psychological counseling, and all kinds of advice – including on mental health.

This is even more important as we confront a national mental health crisis. The National College Health Assessment[10] found that 87% of students felt overwhelmed, 85% felt exhausted, 69% felt very sad, 64% felt overwhelming anxiety, and 63% felt very lonely. In the face of this, some students may be less likely to seek help. Students of color,[11] international students,[12] and first-gen students[13] are each about half as likely to seek help as their counterparts.

There are lots of different ways to check in on yourself to see how you are doing; for instance, take some quiet time to breathe and reflect or take an assessment online, such as the "Wellness Quotient," which shows whether your level of stress, diet, activity, rest, and environment are in balance.[14]

A one-on-one meeting with a doctor or nurse can be intimidating, so one idea is to start with a group class or workshop. You can also get in the habit by talking about how you are doing and feeling with a friend. The counseling and psychological services office on most campuses is overwhelmed,[15] so you are better off booking an appointment even before you need it – when the time comes, you can cancel it our use it as a checkup, even if there's nothing urgent.

> ❚❚ There are different options, like getting ten sessions or doing group therapy. I didn't have a great experience at first because my counselor didn't get what I was going through. So, I had to advocate for myself to get a different one, and this was a lot better and really helped me. I highly recommend going to counseling. And it's normal to do it. The stigma for doing it is going away. ❚❚

Tip 37. Ask for emergency aid if you need it.

Colleges are realizing how a small expense can have a big impact. They are also realizing that many students struggle to meet their "basic needs" for food and housing. For instance, the Hope Center for College, Community and Justice found that 45% of students didn't have enough money to buy the food they needed in the last month.[16]

As a consequence, many colleges and universities are providing support for basic needs[17] and emergency aid to help students when unexpected bills or challenges arise.[18] Learn about and use these support services if you need them; you shouldn't have to leave college because of a fine or the cost of travel home in an emergency – or choose between paying for these and the food you need.

Some of the options for supporting basic needs and providing emergency aid include

- Vouchers for campus expenses like books or supplies from the bookstore or meals in a dining hall

- Completion scholarships can cover tuition/fees balances that might prevent you from graduating

- Food pantries to provide food for when you need it, often located in the student union or library

- Emergency loans (that you have to pay back) for when unexpected things happen, like your financial aid is delayed or you have to fly home

- Grants (that you don't have to pay back) in the case of hardship; sometimes these have conditions and sometimes they are unrestricted

Tip 38. Balance work and school.

Many colleges are set up as if all their students are financially supported by their parents or guardians, but the reality is that 49% of college students are financially independent, 64% work during college, and 40% work full-time on top of school.[19]

Balancing work and school can be hard. One student I talked to said:

> *I have to work on top of my schoolwork – I need money for food and housing. It's tough ... Your classmates are working on their classes and you're at your job.*

To balance work and school:

- Try to get an on-campus job, since it will be generally easier to travel to and more likely to be accommodating than an off-campus one, especially if you get an understanding manager who you can ask for help when you need it, like switching a shift.

- Try to keep it below 16–25 hours a week if you can; studies have shown this is the point after which more hours are likely to affect your grades.[20]

- Use your job as an opportunity to meet people, build a support network, have a sense of belonging, and develop yourself as a person and professional.[21]

- See if you can connect your job to your courses in some way; for instance, if you work in a library, you can hone your research skills.[22]

- Check out options for jobs that can be done online, but make sure you're okay working this way and are aware of the trade-offs. It may be more convenient, but you may miss out on some informal interactions that would happen face-to-face, such as getting spontaneously asked to sit in on interesting meetings.

- Become an expert in time management by setting deadlines, planning out your day/week, and sticking to it.

- Develop routines so you don't forget things. This could be everything from charging your technology every night to doing a weekly look-ahead each Sunday night.

Reflection Activity: Feeling Supported

To make the most of this section, you need to reflect on what you've read, commit to some tips to try, and plan to apply them by thinking about what you'll do if you get stuck or have a problem — what's called an "if-then plan."

From what you just read, what might you want to try?

- Ask for help.
- Practice advocating for yourself.
- Work with a student success coach.
- Get a variety of help from the library.
- Go to student health (and not just when you're sick).
- Ask for emergency aid if you need it.
- Balance work and school.

IF: **What might be challenging about using these tips?**

_____

_____

_____

_____

_____

THEN: **What will you do to overcome these challenges?**

_____

_____

_____

_____

_____

START: **What's one thing you can do right now?**

_____

_____

References

1. "How to Design Student Services for Non-Traditional Students," brightspot strategy (blog), April 2, 2019, https://www.brightspotstrategy.com/student-support-services-design-equity/.

2. Charles Duhigg, "How to Win Arguments Like an FBI Hostage Negotiator," Slate, September 27, 2020, https://slate.com/human-interest/2020/09/how-to-get-an-upgrade-tips-fbi-hostage-negotiator-chris-voss.html.

3. "Chris Voss: Never Split the Difference," Talks at Google, May 23, 2016, video, https://www.youtube.com/watch?v=guZa7mQV1I0.

4. Do Good Work Educational Consulting (website), accessed September 30, 2021. https://dogoodworkllc.org/team/

5. "HigherEd Libs Faculty Office Hours," Do Good Work, accessed September 30, 2021, https://www.flipsnack.com/dogoodwork/whatworks-highered-libs-short-version.html

6. Eric P. Bettinger and Rachel B. Baker, "The Effects of Student Coaching: An Evaluation of a Randomized Experiment in Student Advising," Educational Evaluation and Policy Analysis 36, no. 1 (2014): 3–19.

7. "Academic Coaching Student Testimonials," University of Kentucky website, accessed September 30, 2021, https://www.uky.edu/acadcoach/student-testimonials.

8. Krista M. Soria, Jan Fransen, and Shane Nackerud, "The Impact of Academic Library Resources on Undergraduates' Degree Completion," College & Research Libraries 78, no. 6 (2017), https://crl.acrl.org/index.php/crl/article/view/16737/18250.

9. Brent Mallinckrodt and William Sedlacek, "Student Retention and The Use of Campus Facilities by Race," NASPA Journal 46 (1987), https://doi.org/10.2202/1949-6605.5031.

10. "National College Health Assessment," ACHA, accessed September 30, 2021, https://www.acha.org/NCHA/NCHA_Home.

11. "Recommendations for Colleges and Universities to Support the Mental Health of Students of Color," Equity in Mental Health Framework, accessed September 30, 2021, https://equityinmentalhealth.org.

12. Elizabeth Redden, "International Student Well-Being," Inside Higher Ed, May 31, 2019, https://www.insidehighered.com/news/2019/05/31/panel-focuses-mental-health-needs-international-students.

13. "National Data Fact Sheets," NASPA Center for First-Generation Student Success, accessed September 30, 2021, https://firstgen.naspa.org/journal-and-research/national-data-fact-sheets-on-first-generation-college-students/national-data-fact-sheets.

14. "Do You Know Your Wellness Quotient™ Score?" accessed September 30, 2021, https://www.surveymonkey.com/r/WellnessQuotientScore

15. Megan Thielking, "A Dangerous Wait: Colleges Can't Meet Soaring Student Needs for Mental Health Care," STAT, February 6, 2017, https://www.statnews.com/2017/02/06/mental-health-college-students/.

16. Sara Goldrick-Rab et al., "College and University Basic Needs Insecurity: A National #RealCollege Survey Report," April 2019, 54, https://hope4college.com/wp-content/uploads/2019/04/HOPE_realcollege_National_report_digital.pdf.

17. "Research," The Hope Center, accessed September 29, 2021, https://hope4college.com/research-and-resources/research/.

18. Alexis Wesaw, Kevin Kruger, and Amelia Parnell, "Landscape Analysis of Emergency Aid Programs," July 5, 2016, https://www.naspa.org/report/landscape-analysis-of-emergency-aid-programs.

19. "Today's Student," Lumina Foundation, accessed September 29, 2021, https://www.luminafoundation.org/campaign/todays-student/.

20. Catherine Hawkins et al., "The Relationships among Hours Employed, Perceived Work Interference, and Grades as Reported by Undergraduate Social Work Students," *Journal of Social Work Education* 41 (December 2005): 13–27, https://doi.org/10.5175/JSWE.2005.200202122.

21. George Kuh, "What Student Affairs Professionals Need to Know About Student Engagement," *Journal of College Student Development* 50 (January 2009), https://doi.org/10.1353/csd.0.0099.

22. Rosan Mitola et al., "Student Employment as a High-Impact Practice in Academic Libraries: A Systematic Review," *Journal of Academic Librarianship* 44, no. 3 (2018): 352–73. https://doi.org/10.1016/j.acalib.2018.03.005.

5

Building Relationships

Beyond the daily grind of classes and clubs, college is about identity, community, and relationships. It's about figuring out who you are, what drives you, what you're good at, and who you want to be.

It's also about finding out who you want to be with – a community that can support and challenge you, people who can help you see the world and yourself differently so you can make your mark on it. These relationships are also how you learn about and access the resources you need to design your best college experience and build your future.

Finding Community

So many students I talked to had the same advice: "Go to everything." Don't take this literally and burn out, but do start by putting yourself out there. It will be hard and it will be awkward, but it is for almost everyone. It can be as simple as trying something new the first time. If you're living on campus, one student I talked to even recommended leaving your door open so that people in your dorm can drop in. The students all had the same follow-up advice: "Be patient about fitting in." Try to be open and be patient. As you find community, you'll find identity and focus.

Feeling Connected

The good news is that there are lots of low-stakes ways to do this. You can go to a club meeting and not return if it's not a good fit – either way you can enjoy the food! Same for a class. There are orientations and "welcome weeks" set up to give you so many possibilities. Going with a friend or roommate makes it easier too and builds a sense of momentum so the next event or activity you go to gets easier and more enjoyable.

There are also tons of dedicated faculty, staff, and students there to help you; for instance, many professors and staff make a point to put LGBTQ+, first-gen, Veteran Green Zone, and other symbols on their office doors to reinforce that it's okay to approach them and they are your allies.

Tip 39. Focus on belonging.

Feeling supported and connected, feeling that you matter and are cared about, accepted, respected, and valued by a community: these are what researchers refer to as a college student's "sense of belonging."[1]

This is a basic human need and critical to your success in college and beyond. It takes time though, and it's normal not to feel this right away. While "study hard" may be the most universal advice you'll receive about college, "get involved and be part of something" is just as important.

Getting involved will give you a sense of connection to a community, which will make you more likely to graduate[2] and more likely to get higher grades.[3] One student I talked to noted, "When you're connected on campus, you have more access and a network that serves as your support."

Belonging is also a kind of "lens" that you look through as you experience college – it can brighten or darken your view. When you don't feel it, it's likely to reinforce negative feelings such as "This isn't for me."

It starts with finding a college that provides a welcoming, supportive, and caring environment, but it also depends on you. To focus on belonging, put in the time just as you would to study. Dr. Jennifer Keup, the executive director of the National Resource Center for the First-Year Experience and Students in Transition[4] recommends that students do some combination of the following:

- Joining a club, community, or sport
- Finding people through your campus job, one of the "high impact practices" proven to help students succeed[5]
- Using services like tutoring or going to a workshop
- Meeting with your professor(s)
- Connecting with your advisor. There's a strong relationship between students' satisfaction with their advisor and their sense of belonging.[6]

Tip 40. Be patient with belonging.

Focusing on belonging is important. So is being patient, because not feeling like you belong is very common – and it is temporary. Finding community and fitting in are hard for everyone, and you need to know that they do happen eventually. Social scientists have found that just knowing that not feeling like you belong is common and that it's temporary raised students' GPAs, especially among students of color.[7]

> In my first year, it felt like chaos to find my place. It wasn't really until after my first year that I finally had the time to ground myself in my class and my new home. It seems like everyone is doing a lot of socializing, but there's no rush. You try things and it takes time to figure out who you want to spend your time with.

If you are the first, the only, or one of a few students from your family or community to go to college, belonging is even more important – especially since many colleges are still figuring out how to adapt traditions from yesterday's students to support today's students. While it's up to them, finding community and a sense of belonging among other "firsts, onlies, and fews" is key to thriving.

What you tell yourself while you're being patient is also very important. Researcher Terrell Stayhorn recommends: "We believe the stories we tell ourselves.... Feed yourself positive messages: 'I belong. I matter. People care about me. I can do this. I can get help. It gets better.'"

He cautions against the kinds of messages that erode your confidence and become obstacles for you to overcome, such as: "I can't do it. I can't belong. I'm out of place. No one will like me. I won't have friends. This major is not for me. I can't go to grad school. No one in my family has gone to college ..."[8]

Tip 41. Build your support network.

So much of the value of college is the relationships you build with other students, your professors, staff, alumni, and people in the surrounding community. Strong relationships between students, faculty, staff create an environment where you can thrive.

In fact, studies using data from the National Survey of Student Engagement (NSSE)[9] have found that a supportive environment is the greatest predictor of both your overall satisfaction with college and your academic success. Gallup also found that students who felt supported were nearly 2.5 times as likely to prosper in the five areas of well-being they study: purpose, social, financial, community, and physical.[10]

> *I put myself out there to meet new people and talked to them about what I was going through. Now we study together for exams, work on homework, and have a good time when we're not in class. Having a good support system is super helpful.*

To build your support network, Dr. Jennifer Keup recommends that students focus on creating three things:

- *Your "social network"* of people going through the same things as you – students from your residence hall, the clubs you're involved in, your job, and more.

- *Your "peer leader network"* of people who know more than you and may be part of a program your college organizes, like your resident assistant (RA), a peer mentor, or an orientation leader.

- *Your "professional network"* made up of your professors, your advisors, people working in your major/field, and more. This can be very helpful if they belong to a group you identify with; for instance, one student I talked to said: "I joined the Black alumni group and it was great to connect with people who went through the same thing."

Tip 42. Join a living and learning community.

Residence halls that are tied to an idea or interest (like social justice or entrepreneurship) or to an identity (like Latinx, LGBTQ+, or a religion) help bring together the academic and social sides of college. They are also signs that your school is focused on helping students be involved and feel included.

Research studies have shown that students who live in living-learning communities have a greater sense of belonging, an increased sense of social and academic support, more leadership and multicultural experiences, and improved academic performance.[11] Living-learning communities can also be a great way to make a big place feel small.

> *I grew up in a small town and went to a small Catholic school. It was a big jump for me to go to a big school in a big city. It was a culture shock, but you have to be okay being uncomfortable at times, and it's worth it. Don't just do the safe thing.*

The application process for a living-learning community is typically found with other housing options. Get a feel first by talking to members and touring the space.

If your school doesn't offer a living-learning community, you can still get some of the benefit by creating it on your own if you live off-campus with a lot of students in your major or with a shared interest/identity. There are also companies starting to provide this, such as the U Experience, which creates "pop-up" dorms in hotels for students studying online.[12]

Tip 43. Be part of campus life as a commuter.

If you don't live on or near campus, you can still get involved in and be part of the life of the campus. However, in national surveys I've conducted, commuter students tend to be less satisfied than residential students. For instance, compare these quotes from two different student interviews done as part of the survey:

> *I didn't have to build community at school. It fell into place. I did not have to make conscious efforts. It was very natural.*

> *Commuting shuts you out from student life a bit ... I'm only on campus to do coursework and didn't really meet anyone outside my major.*

Try to be proactive and intentional about getting involved and feeling a sense of belonging as a commuter student. For advice on how to do so, I talked to Ayman Siam, a student who created a handbook for commuter students as a summer fellowship project for my educational consulting company.

He recommended intentional networking, going to and organizing your own campus events, making friends with students who live on campus, finding commuter-friendly spaces like lounges and libraries with food and lockers, and venturing out of your comfort zone. The bottom line is don't just go to campus for class and leave.

> *Don't be afraid to talk to people. People are actually generally way nicer than we might think they are. By talking to people, I made new friends, found out about amazing job opportunities and events, and also held deep conversations that helped me understand we all are going through the same struggles.*

Tip 44. Play a sport.

Being part of a sports team builds your community, skills, and satisfaction. A national student experience survey found that student athletes have by far the most positive student experience, with the highest sense of satisfaction, belonging, and feeling supported, as well as the highest levels of risk-taking, growing, teamwork, and over a dozen of our other metrics.[13]

You can play a sport in a variety of ways, whether at the club, intramural, or intercollegiate level (See Tips 122 though 127 on student athletes for additional information). Find the level of commitment and area of interest that works for you. There are also options for students with disabilities who may have limited mobility, as well as eSports.

When you play a sport, remember that college activities are more time consuming than high school. More hours of practice. Higher standards. More competition. Pick the level of involvement that's right for you and know that you might have to give up another activity to do it.

> *I felt at a disadvantage as a first-generation international student. Because I'm here alone, I don't have a lot of connections for my career. Not a lot of people can understand what I'm going through. So, I played a club sport and found a small group of friends that I can talk to, a group where everyone is equal. It's easier to talk to them and I can go to them for advice any time. This was better than just talking to other international students who were as clueless as I was.*

Tip 45. Spend time with people different from you.

It's important to spend time with people like you, who accept and understand you, who create an environment where you can feel safe and be yourself (you can read more about this in Tip 98) and to understand there is diversity in any group of people, even if they "look" the same.

It's also important to spend time with people who are different from you. Decades of research have shown that activities such as talking with students of a different race or ethnicity than you and with students who are very different from you in terms of their religious beliefs, political opinions, or personal values contribute to your success. It has to be a balance though because it does come with risks and comes at a cost; it's harder to be with people who are different but often worth it.

One study found these "enriching educational experiences" to be among the best predictors of success.[14] Others have found that students' exposure to people who are different from them led to their cognitive development[15] and reduced their prejudice.[16]

Look around you. Does everyone look the same? Do they think the same way? Do they have the same religious or political beliefs? Do they all have the same interests? If so, expand your circle to include people who can challenge and support you – and you can do the same for them. When you do this, make sure it's in ways that benefit you and them; for instance, don't burden someone in any kind of marginalized group with explaining and representing the group they belong to.

You can expand your circle in group projects in class, when working on a faculty research project, in club or other student organization activities, or through who you live with. Learn more about cultural competence in Tip 46 and communicating across differences In Tip 47.

Other countries can be more conservative. [Differences are] not even brought up. It can be a shock how open it is here. It makes you think about your own identity. There's not just one way to do things. You get a feeling of freedom and acceptance you've never felt for yourself. You learn to judge people for who they are, not the outside part that culture and society determines.

Tip 46. Assess your cultural competence.

In college, you will encounter lots of people who are different from you. They may come from different places, have different backgrounds, have different beliefs, or may look and act differently than you. To be with and learn from them, you need to develop an intercultural mindset.

Milton Bennett created a model of "intercultural sensitivity," progressing from *denial*, where you don't see differences, to *polarization*, where you judge people based on differences, to *minimization*, where you de-emphasize differences, to *acceptance*, where you really understand differences, to *adaption*, where you can bridge across differences.

Start by learning more about this development continuum.[17] Then see where you are and what you can work on. Your college probably offers the Intercultural Development Inventory as a test you can take to get a sense of where you are in your own development. You can also do this informally by asking yourself some questions and reflecting on how you've handled recent encounters with people who are different from you.

Sometimes this kind of assessment – and the chance to improve your understanding and skills – will be incorporated into a class.

❚❚ *If you want to learn from other people and cultures, take classes on this. Take initiative. Expand your mindset.* ❚❚

Tip 47. Take a workshop in communicating across difference.

One of the best parts of college is belonging and contributing to a community of students, professors, and staff from across the country and around the world. You'll have a lot in common, but also lots of differences. Because of this, how you communicate is critical. As anthropologist Edward T. Hall noted: "Communication is culture – culture is communication."

You need more than empathy for and understanding of people who are different from you. Even with these, it can be very challenging to talk about topics like religion, race, politics, or other things that might otherwise divide us. Differences in the meanings of words, in your tone, and in customs can all get in the way. You need to learn specific communication skills to have these challenging conversations.

Your college's office of diversity and inclusion will offer workshops and seminars that you can bring real-life situations to, and many workshops are offered online.[18] These can help you learn specific techniques as well as principles such as assuming positive intent, checking your own biases and background, and focusing on facts instead of making assumptions.

Tip 48. Be the real you and avoid a "cookie-cutter" identity.

Avoid taking on a cookie-cutter identity among your peers just to fit in. Instead, try to be the real you as you interact with people different from you and be ready to learn and grow.

In his book *The Cost of Inclusion*, ethnographer Blake R. Silver uncovered that in order to fit in quickly, students take on (or get typecast into) typical roles: managers, educators, entertainers, associates, and caregivers. Unfortunately, these roles are neither equally accessible to different students nor equally valued. They also tend to stick with you and define you throughout your college experience.[19]

While playing a cookie-cutter role or adopting this identity can be a necessary coping mechanism at times, make a conscious decision to play different roles in the different groups you are in, from classes to clubs. Be careful about "fitting in" – it's about finding a place where you feel valued and accepted, not about changing who you are to be accepted.

To help with this, reflect on your own identity by looking at a "social identity wheel"[20] and thinking about how your race, ability, religion, and other aspects have shaped who you are today and who you want to be tomorrow. Make space for others too so they aren't forced into a role that they don't want to play or one with less status.

▊▊ Embrace your identity instead of changing yourself to fit in – then you lose yourself. Be proud of who you are. You bring more to campus. In my first-year seminar, it was strange and confusing – my school is a PWI. We had to go door to door in the community for an assignment. My white classmates were scared and uncomfortable, but I felt like I was myself and this helped other students learn. ▊▊

Tip 49. Think about more than yourself.

In his amazing "This Is Water" graduation speech at Kenyon College, late author David Foster Wallace encouraged graduates not just to learn how to think (as you do in college), but to learn how to think about more than yourself.[21]

When you think about more than yourself, you can choose what you pay attention to – and then turn that attention into meaning by choosing what ideas, values, or religion to "worship."

Learning how to focus your attention is what puts you on a path to finding your purpose, making an impact, and making a difference. To put this into practice, look for opportunities to build your empathy by meeting and listening to people who are different from you and engaging in activities such as role play that put yourself in someone else's shoes. Then look for chances to act on this empathy, for instance, for a service learning project like tutoring or volunteering.

We learn a lot in school, and I like to put it out there and use it. I volunteer in a youth group doing workshops, training, and advocacy. I'm learning about myself and issues that are happening at the same time. I can connect with them in a way that's different from an older person telling them what to do.

Tip 50. Lead something.

Whether a class project, club, sports team, or something else, you'll benefit greatly from leading something in college. You'll become more aware and connected, gain communication and problem-solving skills, and make friends while making an impact.

Playing a leadership role in college will not only help you and your teammates while you are there, but it will build confidence, skills, and a network. This will also help you identify and work toward your life and career goals. One study has found student leaders' salaries after college are 7% higher.[22]

Many colleges have a specific office or group dedicated to helping student leaders. These are great places to start and typically offer workshops, coaching, assessments, and training to help you develop as a leader. One way to see how you are doing is the Socially Responsible Leadership Scale (SRLS), which measures things like your self-awareness, commitment, teamwork, and adaptability.[23]

When you are in high school, things are led by teachers and they have the responsibility to make sure it goes well. There's always someone to back you up if it doesn't work. In college, it's up to you. This makes you step up. Putting yourself out there as a leader, someone who's willing to be there for other people, [who] will help you, help you make friends, and help with the transition out of college.

Tip 51. Make a difference in your local community.

"Service learning" activities such as tutoring, mentoring, organizing, building, or other community service activities create opportunities for you to learn and help – building your empathy for others and getting beyond yourself.

Research from the American Association of Colleges and Universities shows that these civic engagement activities have many benefits.[24] Students who participate in them tend to get better grades, be more likely to stay in school, feel a greater sense of commitment to their studies, have a greater connection to their community, learn more, develop greater emotional intelligence, and build essential skills such as communication and critical thinking.

Service learning projects could be anything from a campaign to increase student awareness of mental health to a project to improve a local park to setting up a tutoring program in a local school. They can happen over a weekend or last more than a year. The important thing is they give you a chance to connect with people and contribute.

Most colleges and universities have an office or center that coordinates service learning or civic engagement. These are good places to start. So are centers for leadership and social impact on campus. They can give you ideas for projects, advice on how to do them, and connections to others to do them with. There are also likely local nonprofits or national organizations like United Way.

We are learning a lot of things and sometimes don't know how to apply them. Doing something in the community – like for a class project – makes you feel like what you are studying is useful and makes you feel less hopeless. You have an outlet.

Reflection Activity: Building Relationships

To make the most of this section, you need to reflect on what you've read, commit to some tips to try, and plan to apply them by thinking about what you'll do if you get stuck or have a problem – what's called an "if-then plan."

From what you just read, what might you want to try?

- Focus on belonging.
- Be patient with belonging.
- Find supportive relationships.
- Join a living and learning community.
- Be part of campus life as a commuter
- Play a sport.
- Spend time with people different from you.
- Assess your cultural competence.
- Take a workshop in communicating across difference.
- Be the real you and avoid a "cookie-cutter" identity.
- Think about more than yourself.
- Lead something.
- Make a difference in your local community.

IF: **What might be challenging about using these tips?**

_____

_____

_____

_____

_____

_____

THEN: **What will you do to overcome these challenges?**

_____

_____

_____

_____

_____

_____

START: **What's one thing you can do right now?**

_____

_____

_____

References

1. Terrell Strayhorn, *College Students' Sense of Belonging: A Key to Educational Success for All Students* (Routledge & CRC Press, 2019), https://www.routledge.com/College-Students-Sense-of-Belonging-A-Key-to-Educational-Success-for-All/Strayhorn/p/book/9781138238558.

2. Amy L. Hawkins, "Relationship between Undergraduate Student Activity and Academic Performance," *Purdue e-Pubs*, April 23, 2010, 41.

3. Jing Wang and Jonathan Shiveley, "The Impact of Extracurricular Activity on Student Academic Performance," January 2009, 19, available at https://www.cair.org/wp-content/uploads/sites/474/2015/07/Wang-Student-Activity-Report-2009.pdf

4. "National Resource Center for The First-Year Experience and Students in Transition," University of South Carolina website, accessed September 30, 2021, https://sc.edu/about/offices_and_divisions/national_resource_center/index.php.

5. Alexa Wesley, Alexis Wesaw, and Omari Burnside, "Employing Student Success: A Comprehensive Examination of On-Campus Student Employment," NASPA report, February 15, 2019, https://www.naspa.org/report/employing-student-success-a-comprehensive-examination-of-on-campus-student-employment.

6. Krista Soria, "Advising Satisfaction: Implications for First-Year Students' Sense of Belonging and Student Retention," The Mentor: an Academic Advising Journal 14 (2012), https://doi.org/10.26209/mj1461316.

7. Shannon T. Brady et al., "A Brief Social-Belonging Intervention in College Improves Adult Outcomes for Black Americans," *Science Advances* 6, no. 18 (May 2020): eaay3689, https://doi.org/10.1126/sciadv.aay3689.

8. "College Belonging: Dr. Terrell Strayhorn," *Just a Few Questions* (podcast), January 30, 2021, https://anchor.fm/marc-sims/episodes/College-Belonging-Dr--Terrell-Strayhorn-epn51c.

9. "NSSE's Conceptual Framework (2013)", Indiana University, accessed September 29, 2021, https://nsse.indiana.edu//nsse/psychometric-portfolio/conceptual-framework-new-version.html.

10. Bruno Manno, "Manno: College Is More than a Wage Premium — It's a Road to Well-Being and a Satisfying Life," August 4, 2019, https://www.the74million.org/article/college-is-more-than-a-wage-premium-its-a-road-to-well-being-and-a-satisfying-life/.

11. Lisa B. Spanierman et al., "Living Learning Communities and Students' Sense of Community and Belonging," *Journal of Student Affairs Research and Practice* 50, no. 3 (August 2013): 308–25, https://doi.org/10.1515/jsarp-2013-0022.

12. The U Experience (website), accessed September 29, 2021, https://www.theuexperience.com.

13. "Student Experience Strategy to Support Underserved Students," *brightspot strategy* (blog), accessed September 29, 2021, https://www.brightspotstrategy.com/whitepaper/support-underserved-higher-education-student-experience/.

14. Ernest T. Pascarella, Tricia A. Seifert, and Charles Blaich, "How Effective Are the NSSE Benchmarks in Predicting Important Educational Outcomes?," *Change: The Magazine of Higher Learning* 42, no. 1 (January 2010): 16–22, https://doi.org/10.1080/00091380903449060.

15. Nicholas A. Bowman, "College Diversity Experiences and Cognitive Development: A Meta-Analysis," *Review of Educational Research* 80, no. 1 (March 2010): 4–33, https://doi.org/10.3102/0034654309352495.

16. Thomas Pettigrew and Linda Tropp, "How Does Intergroup Contact Reduce Prejudice? Meta-Analytic Tests of Three Mediators," European *Journal of Social Psychology* 38 (September 2008): 922–34, https://doi.org/10.1002/ejsp.504.

17. "The Roadmap to Intercultural Competence Using the IDI," Intercultural Development Inventory, April 10, 2012, https://idiinventory.com/.

18. "Communication Skills for Dialoguing across Difference," edX, accessed September 29, 2021, https://www.edx.org/course/communication-skills-for-dialoguing-across-difference.

19. Blake R. Silver, *The Cost of Inclusion: How Student Conformity Leads to Inequality on College Campuses* (University of Chicago Press, 2020), https://press.uchicago.edu/ucp/books/book/chicago/C/bo50271509.html.

20. "Social Identity Wheel," LSA Inclusive Teaching, University of Michigan, n.d., https://sites.lsa.umich.edu/inclusive-teaching/social-identity-wheel/.

21. David Foster Wallace, "This Is Water - Full Version - David Foster Wallace Commencement Speech," YouTube, 2013, https://www.youtube.com/watch?v=8CrOL-ydFMI.

22. Sheng Cui, Yangyong Ye, and Xiaojing Zhang, "Uncovering the Sources of the Head Student Wage Premium—Based on China College Student Panel Survey" (European Conference for Educational Research, Hamburg, Germany: European Educational Research Association, 2019), https://eera-ecer.de/ecer-programmes/conference/24/contribution/47459/.

23. "Socially Responsible Leadership Scale," SRLS Online, accessed September 29, 2021, https://srls.umd.edu/.

24. Christine M. Cress, "Civic Engagement and Student Success: Leveraging Multiple Degrees of Achievement," Diversity & Democracy 15, no. 3 (October 2012), https://www.aacu.org/publications-research/periodicals/civic-engagement-and-student-success-leveraging-multiple-degrees.

6

Mastering Technology

There was a time when your experience on campus and your experience online were separate. No longer. Expect these to be intertwined in all aspects of your student life. You'll use technology to find a club. You'll watch a lecture online and talk about it in person. You'll talk to your advisor or therapist by video. You'll use technology to find and reserve a study space. You'll register for classes and pay your bills online.

Getting the Technology You Need

Your college will provide access to desktops, laptops, and other equipment, along with the software you'll need. You can even borrow everything from laptops to chargers to cameras from your library or help desk. You may also bring your own.

Learning to Make Technology Work for You

You'll first need to explore the options to know what's available. Once you understand what's there, you'll need to organize and make sense of it, because it's sprawling, complicated, and confusing. For instance, most schools have a "learning management system," such as Canvas or Blackboard, where you access all the readings, videos, and assignments for your classes and a separate "student information system," such as Banner, Oracle, or Workday, where you access your personal information and grades. The good news is that software is getting easier to use, colleges are bringing different services and features together into a single "portal" for you, chatbots can do the finding for you in many cases, and actual humans can help you if you want!

Keeping Up with Change

But technology is always changing. To take advantage of it, you need to keep learning. Go to workshops to learn specific software, for example, to edit a video or analyze statistics. Get tips from friends to see what apps and hacks they are using. Go to the help desk and ask questions. Take a break and unplug when you get overwhelmed.

Tip 52. Look into what technology will be required.

The high cost of textbooks surprises students and parents. Now it's also the requirements for technology and the cost of meeting them, like buying a laptop and getting high-speed internet.

Check with your school to understand what's required, what's provided, and what they can do to help if you don't have what you need. Most schools have lists of what you need as well as ways to get it from them in a campus store or online, often with a student discount.

The good news is that the COVID-19 pandemic caused many institutions to start asking about students' technology needs and come up with ways to help.[1] To take advantage of these:

- *Talk to your financial aid office* if you'll need to buy a laptop, broadband, or other technology and be sure this incorporated into how they calculate your financial needs.

- *Look for programs that loan out equipment*. Most colleges lend a range of devices, such as laptops, tablets, VR headsets, cameras, and more at their libraries, computer labs, and elsewhere. Many do this for as much as a semester at time, often at no cost

- *Have a contingency plan* so you'll know what you'll do ahead of time if something breaks; for instance, know where the technology help desk is (often in a library) or how to reach them.

- *Plan for times when Wi-Fi isn't working* (or working well enough) by having an adapter so you can plug in to the campus network (or at home).

Tip 53. Organize your time, tasks, and files.

In college you have freedom in what, where, and when you study and socialize — and who you do it with. That means you have to be organized, otherwise time and opportunities will slip away.

One student I talked to observed, "You have to have an organization system. I went into college thinking I'd have more time since I wasn't in class all day, but that wasn't the case." Four important things to organize are

- **Your time:** You'll need a calendar to track classes, meetings, events, deadlines, bills, and more (apps like Clockwise can also help create focus, free up time, and help you reduce distractions).[2]

- **Your tasks:** You'll need a to-do list to keep track of your tasks, such as working on a project, dropping a class, or signing up for an event.

- **Your files:** You'll need to keep all your information organized, for example, with a folder for each class or club and a common structure within each for assignments, readings, etc.

- **Your notes:** You'll need a place to keep all your notes about classes, career, and clubs in one place.

Tip 54. Control your calendar to succeed in online classes.

Once all or part of your learning no longer has a fixed time and place, you have flexibility in where and when you learn. So, you need to be more intentional about how you set goals, manage your time, maintain focus, monitor your progress, and manage your distractions.

Several studies point to the importance of this kind of "self-regulation" as a key to success in learning online.[3]

To control your calendar and online classroom,

- Set goals for yourself and map out the milestones for your courses, such as tests and assignments.

- Decide how and when you'll check on how you're doing.

- Connect your calendar app to the other apps you are using, such as Canvas, Blackboard, and Zoom.

- Block out time on your calendar for readings, lectures, work on assignments, and your work time with your peers based on how long you think they'll each take.

- Designate a place to study where you can focus and create consistency and a routine.

- Be proactive about managing technology distractions by turning off or putting away devices you don't need and even using apps that help you focus, such as Forest.[4]

    ❚❚ *I'm taking eighteen credits. I'm working on campus. I'm working on ten different things outside of classes, so it's super important to manage my time. I use Google Calendar, Drive, and Tasks for everything. Making it fun helps, since it's not, like playing around with different colors and features.* **❚❚**

Tip 55. Find ways to stay informed – other than email.

Every college and university sends their students too much email about deadlines, events, and other announcements. Only 5–10 percent of these get opened, but colleges act as if they all do – and are surprised when students aren't informed.

If they are student centered, they are looking at reducing and coordinating this. For instance, Michigan State found they sent students 1,200 emails in their first year.[6] But even the best still send too much email.

Find other ways to keep up with what's going other than email, including:

- Follow your college (and specific schools and departments) on social media.

- Follow your student government and clubs of interest on social media.

- Sign up for text-based notifications on specific topics, with tools like Remind.[7]

- Sign up for monthly newsletters from your school or department because they are good summaries of what's to come

- Ask your college's chatbot[8] (if they have one).

- Browse physical bulletin boards in key spots like elevators and lobbies.

- Talk to real live humans, including friends, RAs (Resident Advisors), advisors, or the staff in your program/department.

Tip 56. Use your own "workaround" tools when you need to.

Colleges and universities often play it safe when it comes to their technology. They may be slow, have clunky interfaces, or use platforms that don't connect to each other.

You may need to use workaround tools for budgeting, scheduling, or other tasks while colleges catch their tech up to your needs. For instance, Coursicle[9] is a user-friendly course scheduler that students can use to play around with their schedule visually. Group.me[10] is a great way to organize group chats to coordinate and do group work.

A great source of workaround tools are students who are a year or two ahead of you. Ask them about their toolkit and pick a few to try out.

Once you've organized your time, tasks, and information, you can start looking for ways to make your life simpler with workaround tools that automatically connect different apps and information, like Linktree[11] for social media, Charli[12] for files, Clockwise,[13] and Shift[14] for apps. Lots of blogs, such as College Info Geek,[15] review and rank apps for you. Of course, social networking tools can help too.

> ▌▌ *I was an out of state student, the only one from my high school. I felt alone. I'm starting and don't have a social network to count on. So, I added tons of strangers on Snapchat. That was my way to engage and try to meet people. I'm only friends with a few of them years later, but it was great to myself out there. It's okay if you fail and some don't become your friends.* ▌▌

Reflection Activity: Mastering Technology

To make the most of this section, you need to reflect on what you've read, commit to some tips to try, and plan to apply them by thinking about what you'll do if you get stuck or have a problem – what's called an "if-then plan."

From what you just read, what might you want to try?

- Look into what technology will be required.

- Organize your time, tasks, and files.

- Control your calendar to succeed in online classes.

- Check out (and try out) technology.

- Find ways to stay informed – other than email.

- Use your own "workaround" tools when you need to.

IF: **What might be challenging about using these tips?**

_____

_____

_____

_____

_____

THEN: **What will you do to overcome these challenges?**

_____

_____

_____

_____

_____

START: **What's one thing you can do right now?**

_____

_____

References

1. Zipporah Osei, "Visions of a Post-COVID Higher Education Utopia," *Open Campus* (blog), April 24, 2020, https://www.opencampusmedia.org/2020/04/24/visions-of-a-post-covid-higher-education-utopia/.

2. Clockwise (website), accessed September 29, 2021, https://www.getclockwise.com/.

3. Rachel Bradley, "Measuring Self-Efficacy and Self-Regulation in Online Courses," *College Student Journal* 51 (June 13, 2018).

4. "Technology Lending," NC State University Libraries, accessed September 29, 2021, https://www.lib.ncsu.edu/devices.

5. Forest (website), accessed September 29, 2021, https://www.forestapp.cc/.

6. Bridget Burns and Alex Aljets, "Using Process Mapping to Redesign the Student Experience," *Educause Review*, March 26, 2018, https://er.educause.edu/articles/2018/3/using-process-mapping-to-redesign-the-student-experience.

7. Remind (website), accessed September 29, 2021, https://www.remind.com/.

8. Laura Pappano, "College Chatbots, With Names Like Iggy and Pounce, Are Here to Help," *New York Times*, April 8, 2020, https://www.nytimes.com/2020/04/08/education/college-ai-chatbots-students.html.

9. Coursicle (website), accessed September 29, 2021, https://www.coursicle.com/.

10. GroupMe (website), accessed September 29, 2021, https://groupme.com/en-US/.

11. LinkTree (website), accessed September 29, 2021, https://linktr.ee/.

12. Charli AI (website), accessed September 29, 2021, https://www.charli.ai/.

13. Clockwise.

14. Shift (website), accessed September 29, 2021, https://tryshift.com/.

15. Ransom Patterson, "The 25+ Best Productivity Apps in 2021," College Info Geek, October 18, 2019, https://collegeinfogeek.com/productivity-apps/.

7

Enjoying your Campus

When you add up all the residence halls, dining halls, classrooms, labs, offices, and libraries, the average four-year college campus has about 360 square feet for every student. There are lots of spaces for you to use and you'll need to explore it – digitally and physically – to find your niche and take full advantage of it.

Learning about Your Campus

You can use space to find community and resources. You can wander and get "lost" on your own or with friends. You can reserve spaces for a club meeting or to study in. You can spread out to get your laptop, coffee, and notes just right. You can decorate your dorm and move around the whiteboards in the libraries to make space your own. You can even give feedback to improve the campus or give input on the planning of your college's next building (there's always a next building).

Making It Meaningful

Going to places and seeing people creates memories and meaning. One of the struggles of the COVID-19 pandemic has been that it deprived us of this. Hence, every day feels like the next. Take advantage of your campus. A national survey also found that the campus means even more for certain students – compared to the average, students of color and historically underserved students who were satisfied with the spaces on campus were more likely to be satisfied overall and reported higher personal growth.

Going beyond the Campus

As you learn the campus, remember to go beyond it. Start with the necessities of finding a local pharmacy, grocery store, and go-to places to eat. Then learn about the place you're in, its people, and its history. Experience the surrounding environment whether by grabbing a bite, seeing a movie, or going to a park so you don't go to school in a bubble but rather are better connected to the place you're living and learning in. Finally, make it better. Look for opportunities to volunteer whether tutoring local high school students or cleaning up a park on a day of service like Martin Luther King Jr Day.

Tip 57. Seek out spaces that build community.

Feeling a sense of belonging. Getting involved. Studying in groups. Getting support services on everything from data to writing to presenting. Many of the tips already mentioned rely on the spaces around the campus: classrooms, libraries, lounges, residence halls, rec centers, cafés, or quads.

Space meets your functional needs, such as having a quiet place to sit and think or to bring people together. It also plays a symbolic role, sending messages about who you are and what you're a part of. Use space to find community and resources that will support you as you design your experience in college.

It could be living in a residence hall that builds community (See Tip 42),[1] studying and getting help in a library that increases the likelihood you'll stay in college (see Tip 35),[2] going to spaces with holistic support that increases your sense of belonging (see Tip 39),[3] or visiting an identity-based center that makes you more likely to graduate (see Tip 59).[4]

> *Coming in as a transfer student, I knew it was important to find a place where I belonged, where I could anchor myself. I found this in a center for minority students majoring in STEM fields. In this small space on campus, there were printers, computers, places to store my stuff, a kitchenette, and a place to eat. It also hosted social events where I could meet people pursuing different degrees. Having this space on campus was critical to my experience.*

Tip 58. Get "lost" on your campus.

Colleges and universities have tons of hidden gems that you'll only discover if you give yourself time to wander beyond the familiar paths from your dorm room to class to student union and back.

Great places to get lost include the library's stacks, the art museum's galleries, or a building that's home to a department other than yours. This will help you discover new places, people, and programs that can enhance your experience.

You can do this by wandering with a friend, pointing to random spots on the campus map, or even with the aid of a discovery tool that some campuses have, such as Cambridge University's "Space Finder"[5] or the University of Minnesota's "Find a Study Space."[6]

> *I would go to an area [I] don't know with a friend. We discovered lots of spots to study and eat. We'd see posters about events we didn't know about, but they related to what I'm studying. I should have known about them but didn't and wouldn't have learned if I didn't go out and get lost.*

Tip 59. Go to "centers" on campus to find community and support.

Colleges and universities bring together their people and support services into "centers" or "offices" to make them easier to find – both as spaces on campus and sites online. These centers support many different ways that students identify, such as first-generation students, LGBTQ+ students, students with disabilities, student parents, transfer students, veterans, or identities based on culture and race. (Check out Tips 76, 81, 92, 97, 105, 112, and 117 for more on "centers" for specific student identities).

You can use any center you identify with as your go-to to place to find resources and community. Whether you are meeting with someone one-on-one or attending an event, it's a great place to meet other students (and staff, professors, and alum) with shared experiences that can help you feel like part of a community, that you belong, and you're not in it alone.

A center focused on your identities gives you the opportunity to step back and think about the other aspects of who you are – or a safe space to go deeper into what your identity means to you.

As you get comfortable, the center is a great way for you to contribute and lead. You know what the needs and opportunities are, so you may have an idea for an event or program – and may know the right people on or off campus to work with on this.

Tip 60. Go online to book space, technology, and time with an expert.

While colleges have a lot of resources, they are often in demand. Browse the services and get familiar with the systems you use to book them. Unfortunately, at most colleges there are many different systems and may not work together well. A few key booking systems are:

- **You can book spaces,** like a group study room in the library or a meeting room in the student union.

- **You can book technology,** like a laptop, VR headset, projector camera, or voice recorder from campus IT and/or the library.

- **Y***ou can book time with an expert,* like a librarian, tech support specialist, career advisor, subject tutor, or success coach.

You can also show up at a help desk in person and they can help you book space, technology, or a consultation on the spot.

▎▎I set up an appointment with counselors in a career center. Once I met with one person, knowing that there was a whole team of people behind them with different expertise and sensibilities kind of opened my eyes to what they could do, to new possibilities. Treat it as a conversation. They just want to help you. It doesn't have to be too formal.▎▎

Tip 61. Choose a hall-style dorm rather than suite-style or apartment-style.

There are three main ways to organize rooms in a dorm, also known as a residence hall: along a hallway, in a suite around a common room, or in an apartment. They all have pros and cons, but researchers have found that rooms along a hall create a "socializing architecture" that makes it more likely you'll interact more, have an increased sense of community, and get higher grades.

- The study "Where You Live Influences Who You Know" found that halls had 10.4 interactions per person versus 8.5 interactions for those in suites.[7]

- The study "Residence Hall Architecture and Sense of Community" found a higher sense of community in halls.[8]

- The study "The Hidden Structure: The Influence of Residence Hall Design on Academic Outcomes" found higher academic performance among students in residence halls (2.9 vs 2.8 average GPA, with even larger improvement of almost half a letter grade among Black students).[9]

Use your campus tour and conversations with guides, admissions counselors, and others to learn about the campus housing options to and how they are organized – halls, suites, or apartments. You can also check out ratings and review sites; for instance, niche.com makes an annual list of the top-rated dorms.[10]

Tip 62. Conduct an equity audit of your college's spaces.

Campuses strive to be welcoming and inclusive places at a minimum. Many now seek to go beyond this to be antiracist places that center on communities that have been underserved.

Students can help their colleges make progress by evaluating their campus through their own eyes and proposing solutions to scale up what's working and fix what's not.

What can you include in your campus equity audit?

- Policies for who gets what space and who has access
- Operations, including space hours and staffing
- Legacies and histories of space
- Imagery and symbols within the space
- Proportions, layouts, and locations of space
- Furniture and equipment within spaces
- Which programs and events can occur in a space
- Who's involved in planning and design of spaces
- How the planning process is facilitated

One great example of this is the Space Matters initiative[11] at Portland Community College, and a great resource is Equity-Centered Community Design,[12] created by Creative Reaction Lab.

Tip 63. Use your campus for what you can't do online.

One of the lessons of the COVID-19 pandemic is that everyone learned to do more online but also learned how much more we value being together in person – and that there are some activities that you can't do as well (or at all) online.

Spend your time doing things that take full advantage of the campus. This won't include sitting in a large auditorium listening to a professor's lecture that probably would have been better to watch, pause, discuss, and watch again online. Instead, consider things like

- Working in a laboratory (see more on this in Tip 29).

- Sports, exercise, and recreation (see more on this in Tip 44).

- Making things in a studio or shop (see more on this in Tip 26).

- Dance, drama, or other kinds of performances.

- Wandering or exploring a place without a purpose or agenda (see more on this in Tip 58).

- Doing a service learning or class project with a local organization, such as a nonprofit or school (see more on this in Tip 51).

Tip 64. Use space as a tool for memory, identity, and belonging.

Spaces like your room can do more than store your stuff and help you do stuff like sleep and study. Use your space (and the ones you go to) to help you recall what you need to know, remind you who you are, and remember what you're a part of.

Space is an example of what philosopher and cognitive scientist Andy Clark called the "Extended Mind" – a tool we can think with beyond our brains and body.[13]

Your space can be a tool for memory – a place to hang things like a calendar or sticky notes, to keep important deadlines or important concepts in visible places.

It can be a tool for identity – a place to display things that are important to you, things that make you who you are, such as pictures of family or places you've been, awards, or maps.

Space can be a tool for belonging too – a place to exhibit groups you are a part of, whether it's your family and friends, a club, a team, or even your major.

❚❚ There are so many international students from so many different places, it can be hard to find a space that resonates with you on campus. So, go off campus as well, for instance, [to] restaurants and supermarkets. Be a part of the community. It's great to overhear someone else speaking your language. They remember your face and your order and it feels like home. ❚❚

Tip 65. Make the most of your commute to campus.

Many students live locally and commute to campus for classes and club activities. Your commute can be wasted time that you dread, or you can find ways to minimize the stress of it and make the most of your experience in transit.

To help you make it a positive experience, I talked to Ayman Siam, a student who created a handbook for commuter students as a summer fellowship project for my educational consulting company. He offered two bits of advice:

- *To minimize the stress of your commute*, make your own schedule, leave early, know alternate routes, be aware of your aware of your surroundings, memorize your class schedule, meditate, listen to music/audiobooks/ podcasts, and learn about places to eat on/around campus.

- *To make the most of your experience in transit*, get really good at time management (see Tip 54), do class readings, review class notes, check your email before class, and you can even watch class videos/lectures (when you have a signal).

  My commute to school back and forth is over three hours on the subway. To better use my time, I go over my class notes for the day, read the news, or listen to podcasts/audiobooks.

(And once you are on campus, take advantage of commuter-friendly spaces where you can camp out, meet people, and get things done. These might be a commuter's lounge in the student union, a library, or an identity center that typically has study space, cafés or food prep areas with vending/microwave/ fridge, and lockers.)

Reflection Activity: Enjoying Your Campus

To make the most of this section, you need to reflect on what you've read, commit to some tips to try, and plan to apply them by thinking about what you'll do if you get stuck or have a problem — what's called an "if-then plan."

From what you just read, what might you want to try?

- Seek out spaces that build community.
- Get "lost" on your campus.
- Go to "centers" on campus to find community and support.
- Go online to book space, technology, and time with an expert.
- Choose a hall-style dorm rather than suite-style or apartment-style.
- Conduct an equity audit of your college's spaces.
- Use your campus for what you can't do online.
- Use space as a tool for memory, identity, and belonging.
- Make the most of your commute to campus.

IF: **What might be challenging about using these tips?**

_____

_____

_____

_____

_____

THEN: **What will you do to overcome these challenges?**

_____

_____

_____

_____

START: What's one thing you can do right now?

_____

_____

_____

References

1. Ann Sloan Devlin et al., "Residence Hall Architecture and Sense of Community: Everything Old Is New Again," *Environment and Behavior* 40, no. 4 (July 1, 2008): 487–521, https://doi.org/10.1177/0013916507301128.

2. Krista M. Soria, Jan Fransen, and Shane Nackerud, "The Impact of Academic Library Resources on Undergraduates' Degree Completion," *College & Research Libraries* 78, no. 6 (2017), https://crl.acrl.org/index.php/crl/article/view/16737/18250.

3. S. D. Museus, V. Yi, and N. Saelua, "How Culturally Engaging Campus Environments Influence Sense of Belonging in College: An Examination of Differences between White Students and Students of Color," *Journal of Diversity in Higher Education* 11, no. 4 (2018): 467–483, https://doi.org/10.1037/dhe0000069.

4. "Evaluation Shows U of M Student Parent HELP Centers' Positive Effects on Undergraduate Student Parent Academic Outcomes," University of Minnesota News and Events, July 31, 2021, https://twin-cities.umn.edu/news-events/evaluation-shows-u-m-student-parent-help-centers-positive-effects-undergraduate-student.

5. Spacefinder (website), accessed September 29, 2021, https://spacefinder.lib.cam.ac.uk/.

6. University Services – Study Space, accessed September 29, 2021, https://studyspace.umn.edu/.

7. A. Brandon, J. B. Hirt, and Tracey Cameron, "Where You Live Influences Who You Know: Differences in Student Interaction Based on Residence Hall Design," *Journal of College and University Student Housing* 35 (January 2008): 62–79.

8. Ann Sloan Devlin et al., "Residence Hall Architecture and Sense of Community: Everything Old Is New Again," *Environment and Behavior* 40, no. 4 (July 2008): 487–521, https://doi.org/10.1177/0013916507301128.

9. Joshua Brown, Fred Volk, and Elisabeth M. Spratto, "The Hidden Structure: The Influence of Residence Hall Design on Academic Outcomes," *Journal of Student Affairs Research and Practice* 56, no. 3 (May 2019): 267–83, https://doi.org/10.1080/19496591.2019.1611590.

10. "2022 Best College Dorms in America," Niche, accessed October 30, 2021 https://www.niche.com/colleges/search/best-college-dorms/

11. "Space Matters: Race, Equity and The PCC Landscape," Effective Change Agent, accessed September 29, 2021, https://ecapdx.weebly.com/space-matters-race-equity-and-the-pcc-landscape.html.

12. "A Method for Co-Creating Equitable Outcomes," Creative Reaction Lab, accessed September 29, 2021, https://www.creativereactionlab.com/our-approach.

13. Larissa MacFarquhar, "The Mind-Expanding Ideas of Andy Clark," *The New Yorker*, March 26, 2018, https://www.newyorker.com/magazine/2018/04/02/the-mind-expanding-ideas-of-andy-clark.

8

Exploring Career Paths

We're all looking for a career that combines something we care about, something we're good at, and something that makes a positive impact in the world. The trick is how to balance exploring and focusing to get there. Your time in college is a great place to do that.

A lot of students say that they don't know what career they want, but a much of the time, this is because they aren't sure how their interests and skills can fit into/make their future career. Exploring and getting advice can help.

Exploring and Focusing

One of the most common regrets I hear from students is not exploring more early on: taking that weird class, learning that language, applying for that internship, going to that club. On the other hand, if you don't eventually find a focus, you may not build the skills and knowledge you need (or may not graduate on time). The good news is that you can change your focus, so better to pick one and change if you need to.

Finding Purpose and Meaning

As you balance exploring and focusing, you can use your potential career path to give your college experience context and meaning. Educational theorist John Seely Brown has long advocated that students should "learn to be" not "learn about" – don't learn about science, learn to be a scientist.

If you can identify a future career (or some possibilities) and a role model (or models), then you'll be in a better position when it's time to do a class project for a local nonprofit or to take a workshop on a piece of software. You'll be able to imagine yourself doing it, and it will make more sense and be more fun – and you'll have bridged your classes and your career, which can unfortunately seem far apart in college.

Tip 66. Narrow your focus toward a major and career over time.

Your college's job is to provide you with pathways to a degree, check in on your progress, and give you advice along the way so that you can graduate on time with a degree, career path, and life goals that match your skills and interests — this is called a "guided pathways" approach.

This approach has been proven to help more students graduate; a study at Florida State showed that students in a guided-pathway model increased their four-year graduation rate from 44 percent to 61 percent[1] from 2000 to 2009. And a study of 29,500 students in 25 majors over 15 years at the University of Minnesota[2] found that students who followed a more common path graduated faster and with higher GPAs. Another study found that students in community colleges whose course loads comprised at least 60 percent career-focused classes by their second semester were more likely to graduate on time.[3]

It's up to you to reflect on your skills and interests, start focusing, and think hard about the classes you take to ensure they'll help you progress, even if you aren't totally set on a major. For example, maybe you're interested in people — you can take classes in psychology, anthropology, or sociology that will move you in the right direction. Developing focus — even if you change it — will also help you stand out, whether you're applying for a scholarship, internship, or job.

If you're still in love with your major and willing to work hard at it, then keep going. See other people that are passionate about it — do you feel the same way? If not, maybe it's time to venture out. Ask yourself about whether your expectations are set by your parents or this is something you want to dive deeply in.

Tip 67. Find a role model to emulate and write your own story.

Connecting with someone whose work you admire will enable you to explore how they got where they are and help you chart your path.

The graduation rate at CUNY's Guttman Community College is twice the national average; one reason why is that students take a two-part course called the "Ethnographies of Work," where they investigate a range of careers.[4]

To study a potential role model by shadowing or interviewing them, you can look to alumni, companies, and nonprofits that are already connected to your school. Social media can be a good way to identify someone (or a role they play).

Use what you learn from this shadowing and from class projects, internships, and advisors to think about your future. Educator Carol Brandt encourages students to think of career planning as a creative writing exercise where students imagine their future – and rewrite their story as they learn.

> *I used mentors a lot in college. I looked for it in everyone and every interaction, in many ways. Short-term and long-term.... I worked at the career center and my boss became a mentor and role model for me. She welcomed me and spoke to my life at the present moment. It was inspiring to connect with another creative person. I could email her, text her, or make a formal appointment to get on her calendar because we built a long-term relationship.*

Tip 68. Build the skills that employers want most and capture them in a portfolio.

While the skills you need can vary by major and career, many are foundational, such as the five Cs: creativity, critical thinking, collaboration, communication, and computation.

One of the many ongoing studies on this is the American Association of Colleges and Universities' "What Employers Want," which tracks these skills over the last fifteen years.[5] Classes, club activities, and internships are all good ways to build these skills and prioritize the ones you see your role models and mentors using.

As you think about skills, it's important to do your research here and get beyond the hype; for instance, many students dismiss a liberal arts major such as sociology and think they have to major in business for college to pay off. However, researchers at Georgetown University have found that while salary may be initially lower, a liberal arts education does pay off in the long term.[6]

As you learn how to work on a team, analyze data, write well, think creatively, and present your ideas, be sure to capture these in a project portfolio that you can use to communicate your experience to employers. This could be a personal website, using an online portfolio platform like Behance, or a print portfolio you design.

No matter the format, use this as a way to show what you can do and provide examples of how you can contribute in the future. Get in the habit of updating this portfolio every semester because your skills and work will evolve and expand. This portfolio can be part of the online profile you build on sites like LinkedIn to help you pursue an internship or a job – your career services / development office can often help with this.

A portfolio is a conversation starter during an interview. It gives you an opportunity to explain how you use creative thinking and show how you could use your skills on the job. You can prove the way that you think in a visual way.

Tip 69. Seek out "real-world" learning experiences while you're in college.

Internships, externships, or other kinds of experiential learning, such as a class project for a local nonprofit or a co-op with a company, have a lot of benefits. They enable you to apply what you're learning in class to interact with potential role models, learn transferable skills, and to build a portfolio for future career opportunities.

According to the Gallup-Purdue Index, students who had an internship that "allowed them to apply what they were learning in the classroom" were 1.8 times more likely to be involved in, enthusiastic about, and committed to their work.[7]

Experiential learning opportunities can come through formal programs through your career services office or you can seek them out via your professors or others. Alumni are a good place to start, especially those that you have a shared connection with like having the same major, playing the same instrument, being in the same club, or playing the same sport. Many alumni offices use a platform called Handshake to connect students to internships and jobs, and so it's worth getting familiar with it early on.

▌▌ My school has opportunities to work in teams on real projects for companies. It was great to have opportunities to apply what I'm learning and really get to work hands-on on a big project. There are also internships and volunteering. Even if you don't get the internship, it's useful to apply and talk to them. ▌▌

Tip 70. Check up on your career twice a year.

In his book *Think Again*, Wharton professor and organizational psychologist Adam Grant recommends a biannual check-in on your goals and the progress you are making toward them (and there's more about setting goals in Tip 18).[8]

Not only will this force you to create goals and a sense of focus, but it will also help you reflect and decide if you should change course: maybe you are a different person from when you set the goals or maybe you've learned a lot and reached a plateau.

Your career services office would absolutely love you to visit. Sign up for a remote or in-person consultation, and when you do, ask if there are any assessments you can do or questions to ponder in advance. You can also get their advice on how to build your online profile for sites like LinkedIn to support your search for an internship, fellowship, or job opportunity.

> ❚❚ You don't have to have it all figured out. It's okay to change your mind. It's okay to change your major. It's okay to not do what your parents told you to do. You have to have an open mind and explore. Things will find you if you put yourself out there – things you wouldn't have thought to do. ❚❚

Tip 71. Be an entrepreneur.

Bringing an idea to life can be a rewarding experience that helps you explore an interest or career, make a difference, and build skills like creativity, flexibility, and risk-taking.

College is a great time to do this because you're surrounded by a ton of support, including great students and professors to work with, grants and other funding, mentoring programs, workshops to build skills, and events.

Ideas come in different shapes and sizes. You don't have to create an app with millions of uses to make a difference. You don't have to be a business major. You don't have to fit a "typical" mold either; for instance, coming out of the pandemic, Black women are starting businesses at a faster rate than any other demographic group.[9] In fact, your idea doesn't even have to be about starting a company. It might be about starting a film series of a volunteer project.

Check out your college's entrepreneurship center and entrepreneurship club as a place to start. Many campuses also have "incubators" to help you develop your idea, such as the University of Rochester's iZone,[10] or the Blackstone Launchpads[11] on campuses around the country.

I worked in a student-led group that did pro bono design projects for nonprofits and community groups. It was great to work with actual clients who would give us feedback on what we did. This experience helped me stand out and got me an internship. It doesn't have to be directly tied to your major either, something related can be helpful too.

Tip 72. Create a short, straight line between your experience and whatever job you apply for.

Anyone who wants to hire you for an internship, fellowship, or job has to imagine how you'll do on the job in the future based on your past.

Interview techniques are getting better at reducing bias and understanding how you might perform in the future. One technique used is "behavioral interviewing," where you're asked how you'd handle a hypothetical situation.

Employers still have to draw a line between what you've done and what you'll do. Your job is to make this the shortest, straightest line possible so it's easy for them to imagine.

Some of the best ways to do this are to

- Assemble a portfolio of your class projects so you can show how you've solved problems similar to what you'll be facing in the future (More on building a portfolio in Tip 68).

- Be explicit about what skills you've learned and relate them to the position description; for example, design thinking (Tip 22) or data analysis and visualization (Tip 21)).

- Do your research and then make your "elevator pitch" by describing your experience, skills, and objectives in their words.

Reflection Activity: Exploring Career Paths

To make the most of this section, you need to reflect on what you've read, commit to some tips to try, and plan to apply them by thinking about what you'll do if you get stuck or have a problem – what's called an "if-then plan."

From what you just read, what might you want to try?

- Find a role model to emulate and write your own story.
- Narrow your focus toward a major and career over time.
- Build the skills that employers want most and capture them in a portfolio.
- Seek out "real-world" learning experiences while you're in college.
- Check up on your career twice a year.
- Be an entrepreneur.
- Create a short, straight line between your experience and whatever job you apply for.

IF: **What might be challenging about using these tips?**

_____

_____

_____

_____

_____

THEN: **What will you do to overcome these challenges?**

_____

_____

_____

_____

START: **What's one thing you can do right now?**

_____

_____

References

1. Tiffany Fishman, Jen Tutak, and Allan Ludgate, "Success by Design: Improving Outcomes in American Higher Education," Deloitte Insights, March 16, 2017, https://www2.deloitte.com/us/en/insights/industry/public-sector/improving-student-success-in-higher-education.html.

2. Sara Morsy, "Data-Driven Methods for Course Selection and Sequencing" (PhD diss., University of Minnesota, 2019), https://conservancy.umn.edu/bitstream/handle/11299/206428/Morsy_umn_0130E_20206.pdf.

3. Samuel S. Rowell, "Career-Focused Course Sequencing and Retention to Graduation in a Tennessee Community College" (PhD diss., East Tennessee State University, 2015), https://dc.etsu.edu/etd/2542/

4. "Ethnographies of Work," Guttman Community College, accessed September 29, 2021, https://guttman.cuny.edu/faculty-staff/center-on-ethnographies-of-work/ethnographies-of-work/.

5. Kisha Mason, "2021 Report on Employer Views of Higher Education," Association of American Colleges & Universities, March 30, 2021, https://www.aacu.org/2021-report-employer-views-higher-education.

6. "Liberal Arts Education Pays Off in the Long Term, Georgetown Report Finds," Georgetown University, January 17, 2020, https://feed.georgetown.edu/access-affordability/liberal-arts-education-pays-off-in-the-long-term-georgetown-report-finds/.

7. "The Gallup-Purdue Index 2015 Report," Gallup, https://www.gallup.com/services/185924/gallup-purdue-index-2015-report.aspx?_ga=2.163293116.1029449328.1637111356-1043571170.1637111356

8. "Think Again, the Latest Book from Adam Grant," Adam Grant, September 22, 2020, https://www.adamgrant.net/book/think-again/.

9. "Two Indicators: Women and Work," NPR, September 17, 2021, https://www.npr.org/transcripts/1038307729.

10. "IZone," Barbara J. Burger iZone, accessed September 29, 2021, https://izone.lib.rochester.edu/.

11. "Blackstone LaunchPad: Entrepreneurship Training for Students," Blackstone Launchpad, accessed September 29, 2021, https://www.blackstonelaunchpad.org/.

Part 3

Specific Advice to Meet Different Needs

Introduction to Part 3

While I've learned a lot working with over a hundred colleges and universities over the years and in my research for this book, I don't identify as or have much personal experience related to the chapters in this section. I wasn't a student-athlete or a student of color or a student with children. I don't have a disability. I wasn't the first in my family to graduate from college. I wasn't an international student in the U.S. or a transfer student. I didn't serve in the armed forces.

Instead of relying on my own experience and identity, these chapters grew out of my conversations with experts in each area and students who have the lived experience with the challenges and successes you might experience if you share one of these identities – and even if you don't. You'll hear from them directly throughout this section and you can dig into their own research in the references at the end of each chapter.

I am grateful for and indebted to all these contributors not only for providing insights and ideas – many of which became tips in these chapters – but also for identifying specific topics where research studies can give proven practices to help students learn, grow, belong, and succeed.

I'm not telling you how to feel. I'm also not telling you that college is fair. In many ways, the chapters in Part 3 reveal that higher education is catching up to who students are and how to best support all students – and to take a "whole student" approach. It's up to colleges to level the playing field.

There are some things you can do in the meantime to better your chances to learn, grow, and belong. That's what you'll find in the chapters that follow as I share the experiences and expertise from people who can help. Neither these identities nor the tips are comprehensive, but they are a start.

As with Parts 1 and 2, all the tips may not apply to you, and so you might want to skip around and choose the ones that reflect you. However, unlike Parts 1 and 2, there is an added benefit to reading the chapters that at first may seem like they do not apply to you: you'll get a chance to understand what other students might be going through, and a tip for them might just help you too!

9

First-Generation Students

The definition of what it means to be a first-generation student is complex – it can include students without a parent or guardian who *attended* college or without a parent who *graduated* from college. It gets more complicated when you include schools outside the US. Students without a parent or guardian who graduated college in the US are counted as first generation by the federal government, and by that standard, more than a third of students are first-generation students.[1]

To help understand the complexities of the first-generation student experience in this chapter, I spoke with Deana Waintraub Stafford, the director of NASPA's Center for First-Generation Student Success, a great source of information on research about first-generation students.[2] Among all her great observations and advice, she noted:

> ▌▌ The 'hidden curriculum' is what colleges and universities expect everyone knows – that you go to office hours to speak with a professor or instructor – but first-generation students encounter barriers in the jargon, like knowing what office hours are and how/when to utilize them. ▌▌

Challenges for First-Gen Students

Just like the definition, being a first-generation student is complex too. You may also identify with other characteristics, such as being a veteran or having kids of your own. It's also complex because first-gen students tend to have more responsibilities in their family than continuing generation students; for instance, first gens may take care of siblings, contribute financially (most work 20 hours a week), act as a translator, or help the family navigate in other ways. Those ties complicate things because they can make it harder for you to focus on school at a time when it's already hard because you're figuring it all out.

Building on Your Strengths as a First-Gen Student

The good news is that while you've proven your resilience and independence to get this far, you don't have to figure it all out yourself. Without a parent to tell you how it's going to be at college, you're probably used to doing it all yourself, but you don't have to. Your college has a ton of resources to help you, likely in a center for or office of first-generation students. Go there. Ask for help, because you don't know what you don't know. When you go and connect with staff, professors, and other students, the connections you make will help you join a community too. First-gen students are less likely to feel like they belong, but you do, and meeting others will help.

Tip 73. Look for a college that's first-gen friendly.

While all colleges and universities welcome first-generation students, some are more attuned to your needs than others.

Here are some things to look for:

- Is it recognized as focused on first-generation students through a program like the NASPA (the National Association of Student Affairs Professionals) "First Gen Forward"?

- Does it provide a dedicated first-generation center or office that provides resources and community?

- Does it provide specific first-generation orientation and other programs geared specifically at addressing challenges first-gen students may have?

- Is it listed on college search sites as first-gen friendly, such as a "Best Colleges" list?[3]

Once you identify these traits in selecting a school, be sure you take advantage of them by going to programs, meeting with people, and using the services they've received awards or recognition for.

You need to align on culture fit, major, and price of your school. I was at a top state school and left that because I couldn't find my place.... My high school guidance counselor told me not to apply to college. That's the kind of support I had. So, you have to figure it out. As supportive as your family wants to be, it's not always helpful.

Tip 74. Indicate your first-gen status on your FAFSA.

The Free Application for Federal Student Aid (FAFSA) asks applicants to indicate the highest educational level completed by each of their parents/guardians.

Don't leave this blank. Mark it "high school," "middle school," or whatever option best describes the level of school your parents completed. If they attended some college but didn't graduate, you'd mark "high school."

Your college or university will then use this data to compile a list of eligible first-generation students for outreach about specific services such as advising or scholarships. You risk missing out on services and support if you don't get on the list.

In addition to signaling your first-gen status, it's a good idea to complete a FAFSA even if you are not sure you'll receive or need any financial aid. It takes some time to gather the information you need and complete the form, so plan ahead and leave time to ask questions and get help.

Tip 75. Talk with your family about how your role may change when you're in college.

In comparison to continuing-generation students, first-gen students often play larger roles in supporting their households by working and contributing financially, taking care of their siblings, acting as translators, and more.

First-generation students can talk with family members about what their class and work schedules will be – and may have to set some boundaries regarding their availability and responsibilities (see Tip 14 for more on this).

One way to help is to include family members in orientations and other activities that give them a sense of what college will be like. This can also help reduce families feeling "left out."

> *Don't allow family pressure to get to you. They are proud. You are feeling guilty for leaving them behind. If you tell them you are stressed, the response of 'You got this. You're making us proud. You're making a path' doesn't help – it's more pressure. So, remember you are doing it yourself.*

It's also important for you to think ahead about what will be different and what the trade-offs are. Many first-gen students recognize they are delaying their chance to earn money by going to college instead of going to work. It's also important to realize you'll be giving up some independence too by being in college instead of working and having your own place. Yet another reason that it's important to get the most out of being in college.

> *Students give up so much to be in the space. The cost is so much more than tuition. Autonomy is compromised – you may be living with your parents to save money instead of having your own apartment. So many decisions are based on a cost/benefit analysis. So, you go into business or accounting because material constraints in money and time limit your exploration.*

Tip 76. Go to the first-generation center.

Colleges and universities bring together their people and support services into "centers" or "offices" to make them easier to find – on campus and online.

First-gen centers are a great place to learn about what support services are offered, like coaching, mentoring, and tutoring. Many provide resources like a lending library, supplies, and technology too. In addition to local resources at your school, the center can connect you with information and resources from national organizations like the First Generation Foundation[4] and the Center for First-Generation Student Success.[5]

One student I talked to remarked:

> *There's all these sneaky little centers based around identities that have great resources and events and a community.*

The first-gen center on your campus is also a great place to learn that you are not alone. It will connect you with other first-gen students at events like dinners and workshops so you can get oriented, transition to college, and grow together. Then later, you can mentor other first gens, lead activities, and find other ways to contribute to the center and make it a vibrant and valued place.

Tip 77. Learn the "hidden curriculum."

Unspoken rules and norms make navigating college difficult, especially if you're the first in your family to go to college. Talk with older students, advisors, and mentors, to learn about things like asking questions, going to office hours, or what in the world a "bursar" is (where you paid your tuition bill).

Dr. Buffy Smith's book *Mentoring At-Risk Students through the Hidden Curriculum of Education* provides great advice on how to effectively accelerate learning the hidden curriculum. In the book, Dr. Smith notes how mentors and other advisors to first-generation communities can reveal the hidden curriculum to help level the playing field faster. [6]

> ❚❚ *I learned this stuff on the go. I signed up for community college the Friday before my classes started. So, I didn't have a lot of time to prepare. I got familiar with the campus and the student portal. Orientation helps, but no one is going to tell you everything you need to know, like what does 'R' mean? Why is that Thursday? At first, I made the mistake of not asking questions. I wish I learned about counselors, enrollment services, and financial aid earlier. They are not going to judge you.* ❚❚

Tip 78. Know there's a place for you in college.

Many colleges are still in the process of moving beyond traditions, policies, and processes that were designed for yesterday's students, in order to better welcome, include, and support today's students. When people assume that all students know how college works or that they are studying full-time, it can exaggerate the self-doubt and impostor syndrome that many students feel.[7] First-generation students may experience more. In a national student experience survey, first-generation students' sense of belonging was about 10% less than average.[8]

> I think we all question if things aren't going well or you are lost. But this is part of the process. People around us are in the same boat. Everyone struggles as well. Questioning is a good thing. You don't want to be thirty years old wondering "What the hell did I do the last ten years?"

You are breaking new ground, you are distancing yourself from your family in a new way, and you may even have a kind of "survivor guilt" for getting out to get here.

There are many ways to process these feelings so you can thrive:

- Try to identify what's making you doubt yourself.

- Talk to others about it to find support.

- Be sure to celebrate your accomplishments.

- Remind yourself you've earned it.

- Give yourself a break; don't take it all too seriously.

- Avoid unhealthy comparisons, especially from social media.

- Rewrite your story using positive language/tone.

- Help someone else (which will also remind you how much you have to share).

> Imposter syndrome is real. It's something a lot of first-gen students feel. It's something I've felt. It's gotten better and I feel like I belong where I'm at, but the other day, I had so many assignments … Everything was so much, and in the moment I didn't feel like I belonged. It's okay to be upset, but you can't let it consume you.

TIP 79. Remember you don't have to figure it all out yourself.

As a first-generation student, you are remarkably resilient, having blazed a trail for your family. This has meant figuring so much out on your own, such as applying to schools, picking one, getting financial aid, and getting to campus.

There is a downside of figuring it all out yourself; you can miss out on opportunities for support and community and not get the help you need. For instance, NASPA found the first-gen first years are 54% less likely than continuing-generation students to access student health services.[9] One student I talked to captured this well: "We think we can handle everything on our own. You learn it's okay to ask for help."

Asking for help doesn't mean you've already failed. It's a sign of strength and self-awareness. Look for a happy medium between your independence and asking around for help. Tap friends, advisors, and mentors to understand what's out there and check some of your assumptions; for instance, tutoring is free for all students in college, but you may have assumed you'd have to pay for it. (see Tip 32 for more on asking for help.)

> *You don't have anyone to go to since no one has lived through the process, but there's a lot of resources online – for most of my questions I didn't even have to email or call anyone. When I did, the student ambassadors were great. It was helpful to talk to a peer. Makes you feel like you are not alone. It gives you assurance that you'll be able to thrive.*

Reflection Activity: First-Generation Students

To make the most of this section, you need to reflect on what you've read, commit to some tips to try, and plan to apply them by thinking about what you'll do if you get stuck or have a problem – what's called an "if-then plan."

From what you just read, what might you want to try?

- Look for a college that's first-gen friendly.
- Indicate your first-gen status on your FAFSA.
- Talk with your family about how your role may change when you're in college.
- Go to the first-generation center.
- Learn the "hidden curriculum."
- Know there's a place for you in college.
- Remember you don't have to figure it all out yourself.

IF: **What might be challenging about using these tips?**

_____

_____

_____

_____

_____

THEN: **What will you do to overcome these challenges?**

_____

_____

_____

_____

START: **What's one thing you can do right now?**

_____

_____

References

1. Emily Forrest Cataldi, Christopher T. Bennett, and Xianglei Chen, "First-Generation Students: College Access, Persistence, and Postbachelor's Outcomes," (US Department of Education report, NCES 2018-421, February 18), 31, https://nces.ed.gov/pubs2018/2018421.pdf.

2. Center for First-Generation Student Success (website), accessed September 30, 2021, https://firstgen.naspa.org/home.

3. "The Best Colleges for First-Generation College Students," The Best Colleges, July 23, 2020, https://www.thebestcolleges.org/the-best-colleges-for-first-generation-college-students/.

4. "Supporting First Generation College Students," First Generation Foundation, accessed September 30, 2021, http://www.firstgenerationfoundation.org/.

5. Center for First-Generation Student Success.

6. Tyson, Charlie, "The Hidden Curriculum," Insider Higher Ed, August 4, 2014, https://www.insidehighered.com/news/2014/08/04/book-argues-mentoring-programs-should-try-unveil-colleges-hidden-curriculum.

7. "Managing Imposter Syndrome," Husky Experience Toolkit, University of Washington," accessed September 29, 2021, https://sas.uaa.uw.edu/husky-experience/know-yourself/managing-imposter-syndrome/.

8. Elliot Felix, "Five Ways to Better Support First-Generation Students," brightspot strategy (blog), March 25, 2020, https://www.brightspotstrategy.com/first-generation-student-experience-higher-education/.

9. "First Year Experience, Persistence, and Attainment of First-Generation College Students." Washington, DC: RTI International, 2019. https://firstgen.naspa.org/journal-and-research/national-data-fact-sheets-on-first-generation-college-students/national-data-fact-sheets

10

Students with Children

We know from a lot of research that when students don't finish college, it's usually not because of academics. If there are issues with a class or grades, it's usually a symptom of other challenges – not the cause. In fact, by some estimates 40 percent of the reason is financial. While it's up to colleges catch up to who their students are and meet their needs, there are some things that students with children can do to improve their experience.

The Challenges Student Parents Face

Nearly one in five undergrads are student parents[3] (students with children), and they generally have higher motivation and get better higher grades than students without children. But they face far greater obstacles and thus have lower graduation rates. Sometimes the obstacles are psychological, such as a guilty feeling for doing something for themselves.[4] Student parents have more responsibilities outside of school and more to balance, with less time to do so.

I'm a dad, and our three- and six-year-olds can be a handful. I can only imagine how difficult it would be to also be in college while taking care of young kids. So, for this chapter, I spoke to Chaunté White from the Institute for Women's Policy Research (IWPR),[5] and I really appreciate her insights and perspective. She pointed out:

> *Student parents are motivated and highly capable, but the higher education system was not developed with them in mind.... With the right supports they can overcome barriers and find success.... They need to know to that it is important to ask for help and campus leaders need to do more to identify their needs, provide appropriate resources, and work to eliminate the barriers altogether.*

Succeeding Despite Challenges Outside of School

For student parents, the goal is to either (1) stay on track and graduate, since the chances of graduating within six years is 33 percent for student parents[6] compared to 62 percent nationally,[7] or (2) come back to school after stopping for personal reasons, since 35 percent of the people with some college but no degree have children[8] under age eighteen in their household.

The good news is that whether you are trying to stay in or come back to finish school, you can reach these goals with a supportive school environment. This means programs with flexible schedules day to day and semester to semester so you can go slower or faster. It also means the right support services; for instance, Monroe County Community College found that student parents using on-campus childcare were three times more likely to graduate.[9]

Tip 80. Look for a college that's focused on meeting the needs of student parents.

As a student parent, you already have the motivation and skills to succeed if you can find the right academic program and the support you need. There is a surprising number of resources available at colleges and from state and federal support programs. Colleges are doing better and better at making these more accessible and available, but it does take some looking.

The Institute for Women's Policy Research has great resources and research about supporting student parents. From them, we know that about 22 percent of undergraduates in the US are parents – and of those, 70 percent are women and 42 percent are in community colleges.[10] You can look for and take advantage of your college or university's support resources, including the following:

- Choose flexible degree programs with weekend courses, slower or accelerated programs, and hybrid and/or online formats.

- Use your college's childcare if you can, as this will be more convenient and may be subsidized.

- Look for affordable, family-friendly housing, ideally year-round with features like a playground, green space, in-unit laundry, and even a grocery store.

- Find and use family-friendly campus spaces, such as study rooms in the library that include play spaces for kids.

- Lean on mentoring, coaching, and peer support programs when you need advice or just someone to talk to in order to manage stress.

Tip 81. Go to the student parent center.

Colleges and universities bring together their people and support services into "centers" or "offices" to make them easier to find – on campus and online.

If your school has a student parent center, help center, or resource center, take advantage of it. It's a great place to find and join a community of other students with children as well as learn about and access resources to support you. A University of Minnesota study found that students who had high levels of interaction with center staff were more likely to graduate.[11]

You can use your student parent center to find out what resources are available through school, such as childcare grants. They can also tell you about what social safety net programs are available beyond your school, such as using your Flexible Spending Account (FSA) or getting help on your FAFSA. The center can also be the place to find and meet with peer support groups.

One student parent noted in an interview that their student parent resource center

just opened up this whole window for me. They offer childcare grants, supplies, events for student parents, and babysitting during finals – there was an entire support group that I'd never heard of.[12]

Tip 82. Consult national resources for student parents.

The visibility of the challenges student parents face is growing, and so are the research and support for them. Your institution's student parent resource center can be your first stop and point you to other resources. In addition to the resources your school provides, consult national resources, understand the issues, get ideas, and learn about opportunities for financial and social support.

Great resources include

- The Institute for Women's Policy Research

- The Hope Center for College at Temple University

- The Wellesley Center for Women

- Higher Learning Advocates

- The LAVC Family Resource Center

- Ohio State's annual National Student Parent Support Symposium

- The University of Michigan's Center for the Education of Women

One student reflected on how a suggestion from the student parent center and assistance with the paperwork:

> [It] allowed me to put my daughter into an amazing school that would have otherwise been out of the question for her. I look back on my life and the roller coaster that has been my journey with parenthood and college. I am one semester away from graduation and it has been a long four years. I am finishing my degree in English with a minor in political science, and now I have dreams to continue my education at law school. [13]

Tip 83. Lean on and contribute to peer support groups.

Often the best source of advice and support is other student parents. You'll have a lot in common with them and so you can get through tough spots together and celebrate the bright spots.

Peer support groups can provide advice and information on what's worked for them and what hasn't. You can also work together to tackle a common challenge you're facing; maybe it's pushing back together on a bad policy or looking for nearby daycare options.

You can find peer support groups online and through your student parent center.

For instance, the University of Minnesota's Student Parent Help Center includes a Parents as Students Support (PASS) group, which involves a weekly meeting about topics such as study skills, career, financial aid, stress, and child development. It studied its effectiveness and found that PASS participants were more likely to stay in college, graduate, and earn higher grades.[14]

One center director noted in an interview,

> On a traditional campus like ours, you don't see people with children when you walk around.... Student parents don't bring them to class, they don't talk about it. They think they're the only ones. Now they can see, 'Hey, I'm not the only one.' It's a morale boost.[15]

Tip 84. Ask your school about social safety net programs.

As colleges and universities become aware of how their students' basic needs for food, housing, childcare, and transportation are unmet, they are providing more support on their own and by administering state and federal programs. Ask your student parent resource center, advisor, or counselor about assistance programs. These might include

- Child Care and Development Fund (CCDF), a federal program to subsidize childcare.

- Using the Flexible Spending Account Dependent Care Allowance.

- Locations and hours for campus food pantries.

- Scholarships, grants, and other forms of financial assistance focused on student parents.

- Resources to meet basic needs, such as food pantries and food scholarship programs.

- Emergency aid programs for unexpected expenses such as a fine or travel (see Tip 37).

- Workshops and training, such as those led by the Generation Hope Scholars Program.[16]

One student parent noted in an interview:

> *Graduation wouldn't have been possible without the Student Parent Resource Center; I can't even fathom how I would have made it without the resources they provided.* [17]

Tip 85. Push back diplomatically when policies and processes are outdated.

Unfortunately, many policies and processes in college are outdated because they were designed for yesterday's student: 18- to 21-year-old middle-class students, financially dependent on their parents, living and learning on or near campus, and enrolled full-time.

Since today's students are more likely to break at least one of these "traditional" molds, they can't come to an office between nine and five to sign a paper form.

When you encounter these kinds of challenges, push back diplomatically to see if you can find another way; for instance, say something like: "I would if I could, but I am a parent and I work full-time. Could I sign electronically? Do you have other solutions that could work for me?"

It's up to colleges and universities to adapt to meet the needs of today's students, but you can improve your experience and that of future student parents when you alert your college to policies, processes, and platforms that fall short. Most of the time, you'll find that your college simply didn't know your situation or wasn't seeing it through your eyes and so the problem is solvable, without you having to take time off from work, or worse.

One student parent talked to in an interview about pushing back and advocating for himself said, "I felt embarrassed and had to self-advocate with my department by asking for more time to complete the final exam because I could not take the exam at home without interruptions."[18]

Another student parent reflected on the process and policies that can be challenging for student parents:

Largely, student parents exist in an education ecosystem that was not designed with our needs in mind. It's an ecosystem that often overlooks us or leaves us behind, into which we must find ways to fit ourselves, rather than the system providing the flexibility and accommodations we need. [19]

Reflection Activity: Students with Children

To make the most of this section, you need to reflect on what you've read, commit to some tips to try, and plan to apply them by thinking about what you'll do if you get stuck or have a problem – what's called an "if-then plan."

From what you just read, what might you want to try?

•Look for a college that's focused on meeting the needs of student parents.

•Go to the student parent center.

•Consult national resources for student parents.

•Lean on and contribute to peer support groups.

•Ask your school about social safety net programs.

•Push back diplomatically when policies and processes are outdated.

IF: **What might be challenging about using these tips?**

_____

_____

_____

_____

_____

THEN: **What will you do to overcome these challenges?**

_____

_____

_____

_____

_____

START: **What's one thing you can do right now?**

_____

_____

_____

References

1. "College Dropout Rates," EducationData, accessed September 30, 2021, https://educationdata. org/college-dropout-rates.

2. Melanie Hanson, "College Dropout Rates [2021" Education Data (blog), November 22, 2021, https://educationdata.org/college-dropout-rates

3. Susana Contreras-Mendez and Lindsey Reichlin Cruse, "Busy with Purpose: Lessons for Education and Policy Leaders from Returning Student Parents," *IWPR* (blog), March 16, 2021, https://iwpr.org/iwpr-issues/student-parent-success-initiative/busy-with-purpose-lessons-for-education-and-policy-leaders-from-returning-student-parents/.

4. Ross E. O'Hara, "Supporting Student Parents' Success in College," Psychology Today, July 7 2020, https://www.psychologytoday.com/us/blog/nudging-ahead/202007/supporting-student-parents-success-in-college.

5. Institute for Women's Policy Research (website), accessed September 30, 2021, https://iwpr.org/.

6. Barbara Gault et al., "4.8 Million College Students Are Raising Children," IWPR (report #C424), November 17, 2014, https://iwpr.org/iwpr-issues/student-parent-success-initiative/4-8-million-college-students-are-raising-children/.

7. "NCES Fast Facts: Graduation Rates," National Center for Education Statistics, accessed September 30, 2021, https://nces.ed.gov/fastfacts/display.asp?id=40.

8. Catherine Hensly, Chaunté White, and Lindsey Reichlin Cruse, "Re-Engaging Student Parents to Achieve Attainment and Equity Goals," IWPR (report #C501), July 8, 2021, https://iwpr.org/iwpr-issues/student-parent-success-initiative/re-engaging-student-parents-to-achieve-attainment-and-equity-goals/.

9. Lindsey Reichlin Cruse, Barbara Gault, and Jooyeoun Suh, "Time Demands of Single Mother College Students and the Role of Child Care in Their Postsecondary Success," IWPR (report #C468), May 10, 2018, https://iwpr.org/iwpr-general/time-demands-of-single-mother-college-students-and-the-role-of-child-care-in-their-postsecondary-success/.

10. "Student Parent Success Initiative Archives," IWPR (blog), accessed September 30, 2021, https://iwpr.org/category/iwpr-issues/student-parent-success-initiative/.

11. "Evaluation Shows U of M Student Parent HELP Centers' Positive Effects on Undergraduate Student Parent Academic Outcomes," University of Minnesota, July 31, 2020, https://twin-cities. umn.edu/news-events/evaluation-shows-u-m-student-parent-help-centers-positive-effects-undergraduate-student.

12. "Student Parent Resource Center Offers Wealth of Resources," MSUToday, September 1, 2021, https://msutoday.msu.edu/news/2021/student-parent-resources.

13. "Madison's Success Story," UMSL, accessed September 30, 2021, https://www.umsl.edu/studentadvocacy/studentparents/madison.html.

14. "University of Minnesota - Student Parent Help Center," Wilder Foundation, May 8, 2020, https://www.wilder.org/wilder-research/research-library/university-minnesota-student-parent-help-center.

15. "Strategies for Student-Parent Success at the University of Alabama," Association of American Colleges & Universities, May 2014, https://www.aacu.org/campus-model/strategies-student-parent-success-university-alabama.

16. "Resources and Workshops," Generation Hope, accessed September 30, 2021 https://www. generationhope.org/resources-workshops.

17. "Student Parent Resource Center Offers Wealth of Resources."

18. "Student Parent Resource Center Offers Wealth of Resources."

19. Lesley del Rio, "One Student Parent Shares the Impact of the Crisis," *Imaginable Futures* (blog), accessed September 30, 2021, https://www.imaginablefutures.com/learnings/guest-blog-one-student-parent-shares-impact-crisis/.

11

Students with Disabilities

The Americans with Disabilities Act defines a disability as a physical or mental impairment that substantially limits one's major life activity. According to the National Center for Education Statistics, 19% of undergraduate students report they have a disability.[1] Maybe you are visually impaired, deaf or hard of hearing, or are on the autism spectrum; maybe you have ADHD, dyslexia, a physical disability, a learning disability, or a combination of these.

Finding the Best School for You

I don't have firsthand experience with a disability that limited my studies. So, for this chapter, I spoke with Tim Montgomery, the director of Student Disability Services at the University of California–San Francisco,[2] and I'm grateful for his contributions. He pointed out that whatever your disability is, the right school can help you succeed, saying,

> *Students are concerned about getting in and going to the 'best school,' but really the 'best school' is the one that meets your needs and works for you.... There is so much support available that many students don't realize.*

Finding the Support to Thrive

While the government may define a disability in term of how it limits you, colleges and universities can provide a range of adjustments or accommodations to help you thrive. These might include sound amplification, sign language interpretation, accessible facilities and digital spaces, captioning services, course substitutions, note taking services, and more. The important thing to understand is that you are in control and the support you get depends on you. You are the judge of whether your disability impacts you. You decide what you want to disclose, but keep in mind that you have to disclose a disability to get an accommodation for it.

Being a student is complex and challenging for anyone, and all students get a range of support. It's normal to get help – and there's no reason not to. As Tim told me, "You don't get extra points for struggling in silence."

Tip 86. Go to the student accessibility office.

Colleges and universities bring together their people and support services into "centers" or "offices" to make them easier to find – on campus and online.

Your school's student accessibility office or office of student disability services is a great place to learn about what services and supports are available on campus and online, to get help with communicating your needs to professors, and to find people who can support you in learning how to advocate for yourself (and advocate on your behalf).

Many accessibilty offices can be particularly helpful with the transition to college by orienting you to placement exams, housing options, and your school's policies and process – it's really never too early to get in touch.

Some also host events and workshops for you to learn and meet other students. The local resources you find at the accessibility office can also be used in concert with national ones, like the National Center for College Students with Disabilities.[3]

One disability resource center (DRC) shared a student success story:

> *I was raised to work hard and never ask for help, to take pride in what you have done yourself. Yet I found myself needing to ask for help. I felt embarrassed and ashamed to have to ask for help. I felt less than. I dragged my feet at the suggestion from my teachers to contact the DRC. I tried to convince myself that I didn't need to ask anyone for help, that I could just power through this. That was the worst idea I have ever had. Once I had no other option, and was about to fail classes, be put on academic probation, and a slew of other problems, I walked into the DRC.* [4]

Tip 87. Get to know your functional limitations.

Understanding and communicating how your disability specifically affects or impairs your major life activities will help you get the support you want.

Your past strengths and challenges will help guide you into the future. It's also important to remember that things change. What's worked for you in the past may not now; for instance, your classes may be harder than before so you may need more or different support.

To understand your functional limitations, you can

- Identify the name or diagnosis of your disability.

- List any accommodations you've used in the past.

- Reflect on things you've done well versus problems your disability may have created in the past.

- Identify what your situational or environmental triggers might be, especially any changes or anticipated challenges in your environment, such as your support system, access to food/resources, external factors like weather, and more.

- Think about what impact it might have on core activities like listening, reading, writing, moving around, sleeping, interacting, and more.

It's also good to keep in mind that limitations can also be strengths. Students with ADHD are often great at time management, for example. Students with disabilities often get very good at advocating for themselves.

Tip 88. Don't hold back on seeking help.

With a good understanding of your disability and functional limitations, you can seek the support you need. The earlier the better, and the more specific the better.

Don't compare yourself to others; just worry about yourself and what you need. It's all too common for a student not to seek an accommodation because they perceive their disability as less severe than others, but there's no sense struggling in silence.

You can reach out in many different ways, such as by contacting the disability services office or a counseling center. Your advisors, professors, and friends can also point you in the right direction. The important part is don't hold back. You can also learn more about asking for help more generally in Tip 32.

One student shared in an interview:

> My confidence picked up because I knew that I had the office's support and that they were not going to let me become another statistic of someone with a disability not getting an education... My first attempt at college was not a very successful attempt, and that experience stayed with me for quite a long time.[5]

Tip 89. Use disability services in concert with other services.

It's common to get help, whether you are struggling with something or not. Your success in college depends not just on your talent and hard work, but how well you take advantage of the support resources provided.

College is full of support resources to help you conduct research, write well, make a video, build a prototype, find a career path, and more. Disability services are just one of the support services you'll be using to succeed.

Because these support services relate, try to connect the dots. For instance, if you are struggling with writing a paper, disability services can help you overcome your functional limitations while also referring you to other services on campus, such as the writing center, which can help you with the tone, structure, and content.

One student with a disability shared a success story:

❚❚ *Over the years, I have learned that starting an open conversation early makes the class logistics smoother for both the instructor and me. By getting the syllabus early, I can think about accommodations and potential issues.*[6] ❚❚

Tip 90. Take advantage of online classes.

Learning online and at their own pace can help students with a variety of disabilities. This lessens the burden of having to physically get to class when there are a lot of barriers in the way. Recorded lectures enable you to pause, go back, look something up, or even ask a friend you're watching with. Closed captioning can help you follow along. You can "raise your hand" digitally. Chat boxes and discussion boards provide new ways to ask and answer questions.

Take advantage of the online medium as an accommodation for any disabilities you may have and request this as an accommodation if it is not offered.

In a recent story, one student with a painful chronic condition realized that by taking online classes throughout the pandemic, he hadn't missed a single class and noted, "It's helped me realize, like, 'Wait, why can't I get these accommodations all the time? I should be able to attend via Zoom if I need to.'"[7]

More and more courses are offered as "hyflex," meaning they are a hybrid of in person and online, and students have the flexibility to choose what works for them. You can join in real time, in person, or online (often called "synchronous"), or you can work at your own pace watching videos and doing assignments online when it works for you (often called "asynchronous").[8]

Reflection Activity: Students with Disabilities

To make the most of this section, you need to reflect on what you've read, commit to some tips to try, and plan to apply them by thinking about what you'll do if you get stuck or have a problem – what's called an "if-then plan."

From what you just read, what might you want to try?

- Go to the student accessibility office.
- Get to know your functional limitations.
- Don't hold back on seeking help.
- Use disability services in concert with other services.
- Take advantage of online classes.

IF: **What might be challenging about using these tips?**

_____

_____

_____

_____

_____

THEN: **What will you do to overcome these challenges?**

_____

_____

_____

_____

START: **What's one thing you can do right now?**

_____

_____

References

1. "NCES Fast Facts: Students with Disabilities," National Center for Education Statistics, accessed September 30, 2021, https://nces.ed.gov/fastfacts/display.asp?id=60.

2. "UCSF Student Disability Services," University of California San Francisco, accessed September 30, 2021, https://sds.ucsf.edu/home.

3. "National Center for College Students with Disabilities (NCCSD)," NCCSD, accessed September 30, 2021, https://www.nccsdonline.org/.

4. "Success Stories," Disability Resource Center, Bellevue College, accessed September 30, 2021, https://www.bellevuecollege.edu/drc/success-stories/.

5. "Disability services staff help remove barriers for students to be successful," Penn State University, July 27, 2020, https://news.psu.edu/story/626762/2020/07/27/impact/disability-services-staff-help-remove-barriers-students-be-successful

6. "Stories," PACER's National Parent Center in Transition and Employment, accessed September 30, 2021, https://www.pacer.org/transition/stories/.

7. Amanda Morris and Emily Anthes, "For Some College Students, Remote Learning Is a Game Changer," *New York Times*, August 23, 2021, https://www.nytimes.com/2021/08/23/health/covid-college-disabilities-students.html.

8. "7 Things You Should Know About the HyFlex Course Model," *Educause*, July 7, 2020, https://library.educause.edu/resources/2020/7/7-things-you-should-know-about-the-hyflex-course-model.

12

LGBTQ+ Students

According to the National College Health Assessment,[1] about 20 percent of students identify as LGBTQ+. According to a Pew Research study,[2] more than a third of Gen Zers know someone who is nonbinary. For this chapter, I spoke with Genny Beemyn, the director of the Stonewall Center[3] at University of Massachusetts Amherst. I really appreciated the perspective and insights they shared, including this:

> ▌▌ In many ways, the challenges that LGBTQ+ students face are about invisibility – like other people assuming you are cisgender and heterosexual – and about visibility – like other people being hateful and hostile when you are just trying to find a bathroom to use or hold the hand of a same-sex partner. ▌▌

Making Progress, But Unevenly

In addition to growing in prevalence, there is growing but uneven acceptance: now a majority of young people who identify as conservative support same-sex marriage. Federal law prohibits discrimination based on sexual orientation. Now most schools have an LGBTQ+ student group, and the Campus Pride Index rates more than four hundred institutions on their campus "climate" – the attitudes and level of acceptance of students and staff. But progress and acceptance is very uneven from campus to campus, family to family, and depending on how students identify. Small liberal colleges or historically women's colleges tend to be more accepting; on some of these campuses, the majority identify as LGBTQ+.

Invisible and Visible Challenges

For lesbian, gay, and bisexual students, their identity may be invisible; students and professors may assume they're heterosexual and (if they're females) invite them to go "meet guys," which creates an awkward situation or forces someone to out themselves before they're ready. Trans students may experience hypervisibility and suffer hostility and harassment when misgendered by a professor, asked to sign a form or conform to a policy that undermines their identity, or have trouble finding a bathroom they are comfortable in. They can experience increased depression and anxiety as well as less of a sense of belonging.

Tip 91. Learn about your school's climate.

Do your homework as you choose a college and prepare to ask about the campus climate around LGBTQ+ issues and how this may vary depending on your identity.

To better understand your campus climate,

- Call the LGBTQ+ center and ask them, particularly if they have surveys or other measures.

- Look at your college's policies online (but keep in mind, policies don't always translate to climate).

- Look up your school on the Campus Pride Index.[4]

- Look specifically at the trans policy clearinghouse within the Campus Pride Index.

Once you understand the climate, it's also important to think about the support you already have from friends and family.

Acceptance of homosexuality and bisexuality is increasing substantially – but it varies significantly across cultures, regions, and religions. This is generally lagging behind for transgender students who may lose family and/or financial support when coming out or transitioning. So, campus climate may be even more important, depending on your personal situation and plans.

Tip 92. Go to the LGBTQ+ center.

Colleges and universities bring together their people and support services into "centers" or "offices" to make them easier to find – on campus and online.

Researchers have found that LGBTQ+ centers play an essential role on campuses,[5] and there are about two hundred professionally staffed centers in the US.

Beyond learning about resources and events, centers are also a great place to meet other LGBTQ+ students, professors, staff, and alums with shared experiences that can help you feel like part of a community, that you belong, and you're not in it alone. At the center you can also meet allies, learn about advocacy, and get support and ideas about taking care of yourself and your friends.

> [It's] a great way to connect with that community, it's a space just for you. You can meet a lot of people there. My previous college didn't have it and my current one does and it's made a huge difference. I've met more than ten people at the Pride Center in the last few weeks. It makes you feel that you are not alone, that you have a community, that you have a space, that faculty and staff are there for you too.

Tip 93. Be an advocate for change, but not at the expense of being a student.

Part of the college experience is uncovering what you believe in and advocating for what you think is right – and speaking out against what you think is wrong.

Part of identifying as LGBTQ+ often means getting involved and making your voice heard. This can be a great way to find community, build relationships, support each other, and develop your leadership skills. One helpful resource is the "Social Change Model" of leadership, where shared values, a common purpose, and teamwork create positive social change.[6]

But the burden for systemic change cannot fall entirely on your shoulders. Try to find a balance between education and your advocacy. Advocacy can't come at the expense of self-care and being in a good place mentally and physically. If you burn out, you can't help yourself or others.

> ❚❚ *To keep advocacy and studies in balance, I set deadlines and limits, boundaries. My advisors also reminded me that school comes first and when to take a break. Remember that there's only so much you can do, but even the smallest change – like drafting a letter – makes a difference. You can take that as a win. You're not going to be able to change everything.* ❚❚

Tip 94. Find, build, and lean on allies.

Now that you're in college, you need to build your support network – and in turn, support your friends. Some will share your identity and experience. Others will be allies who empathize and stand with you.

With so many new things happening at once – all while you're learning more about yourself – there will be tough, confusing, and stressful times. Who will you go to when a professor misgenders you for the n-teenth time or when your suitemates keep inviting you to meet girls when you want to do anything but?

You can find allies through shared activities for a club, at the LGBTQ+ center, in mentoring programs, or in other settings. Look for people who are willing to listen and learn as well as stand up and speak out. On many campuses, faculty and staff will even signal their support with a sticker/emblem on their doors.

Beyond social support, this can be helpful for classes too. You can speak to other students, advisors, and other professors about which professors are more or less supportive and use this to select classes.

One student noted to Campus Pride:

■■ *Some folks may be comfortable being out in front with all the visibility and attention on them, and others are more behind the scenes. Both are valid and productive ways of being leaders, and I think Campus Pride shows young leaders that allowing yourself the space to become the kind of leader that is comfortable and safe for them is ok.*[7] ■■

Tip 95. Take care of yourself.

LGBTQ+ students tend to experience greater anxiety and depression. Self-care is really important. Think about where you can go and what you can do to recover and recharge. Some ideas include

- Finding a special place on campus where you feel safe and inspired.

- Doing things for yourself to appreciate yourself, such as exercise, journaling, or a hobby you enjoy.

- Establishing a routine that makes recharging automatic and regular, not something extra.

- Seeking counseling or other forms of mental health support.

- Consulting online resources from GLAAD, Campus Pride, GLSEN, and others on the Human Rights Campaign's list.

- Getting involved in your campus LGBTQ+ community through events and initiatives

Stories of self-care[8] **include:**

> *Music is the way that I cope. Zoning out and listening to some of my favorite artists and tracks allows me the ability to zero in on how I'm feeling that day or in that moment.*

> *Most times when I find myself overthinking, I tend to relax my mind by cleaning my environment or my body.*

> *I choose to keep myself safe during this time through spirituality. Each day I do a daily meditation and astral projection activity.*

Reflection Activity: LGBTQ+ Students

To make the most of this section, you need to reflect on what you've read, commit to some tips to try, and plan to apply them by thinking about what you'll do if you get stuck or have a problem — what's called an "if-then plan."

From what you just read, what might you want to try?

- Learn about your school's climate.
- Go to the LGBTQ+ center.
- Be an advocate for change, but not at the expense of being a student.
- Find, build, and lean on allies.
- Take care of yourself.

IF: **What might be challenging about using these tips?**

_____

_____

_____

_____

THEN: **What will you do to overcome these challenges?**

_____

_____

_____

_____

START: **What's one thing you can do right now?**

_____

_____

References

1. "American College Health Association National College Health Assessment II: Reference Group Executive Summary" (Silver Spring, MD: American College Health Association, 2019), https://www.acha.org/documents/ncha/NCHA-II_SPRING_2019_US_REFERENCE_GROUP_EXECUTIVE_SUMMARY.pdf.

2. Kim Parker, Nikki Graf, and Ruth Igielnik, "Generation Z Looks a Lot Like Millennials on Key Social and Political Issues," *Pew Research Center's Social & Demographic Trends Project* (blog), January 17, 2019, https://www.pewresearch.org/social-trends/2019/01/17/generation-z-looks-a-lot-like-millennials-on-key-social-and-political-issues/.

3. "The Stonewall Center," University of Massachusetts Amherst, accessed September 30, 2021, https://www.umass.edu/stonewall/.

4. Campus Pride Index (website), accessed September 30, 2021, https://www.campusprideindex.org/.

5. C. Gilbert et al., "Why LGBTQ+ Campus Resource Centers Are Essential," *Psychology of Sexual Orientation and Gender Diversity* 8, no. 2 (2021): 245–49. https://doi.org/10.1037/sgd0000451

6. Sarah Sheriff, "Social Change Model of Leadership Development," Dickinson College, accessed September 30, 2021, https://www.dickinson.edu/info/20380/student_leadership/3795/social_change_model_of_leadership_development.

7. "Student Leader Spotlight: Vanessa González," Campus Pride, June 23, 2014, June 23, 2014, https://www.campuspride.org/vanessa-gonzales-campus-pride-leaders-in-action-where-are-they-now/.

8. Candace Bond-Theriault, "14 Black LGBTQ+ Folks on How They're Taking Care of Themselves Right Now," SELF, June 26, 2020, https://www.self.com/story/black-lgbtq-self-care-tips.

13

Students of Color

About 45 percent of college students today are students of color: 1 percent American Indian or Alaska Native, 7 percent Asian or Pacific Islander, 13 percent Black, 21 percent Hispanic, and 4 percent two or more races.[1] While there are more students of color and the next generation of students is even more diverse, many students of color do not feel the same level of welcome, inclusion, belonging, and support in college and may not experience the same level of success.

To be frank, I'm white and I don't have lived experiences with this, but it's really important to address, and so I've drawn on experts and people who do have this experience. It's not fair that students of color may face some challenges that white students do not. Some universities are working to change this, and many students are already there advocating for this change. As I mentioned before, I'm not telling you how to feel or that it's fair; I'm providing some ideas for you to consider based on the students and experts I talked to and the research into student success.

For this chapter, I spoke with Dr. Andres Castro Samayoa[2] from Boston College and the Center for Minority Serving Institutions,[3] as well as Dr. Terrell Strayhorn from Virginia Union University and the Center for the Study of HBCUs.[4] I really appreciate their insights.

So much of this chapter is about balancing being with people who share your identities and people who are different from you. Dr. Castro Samayoa summarized this perfectly:

> ▮▮ *Finding communities where you don't have to account for or justify yourself is critical in school and in general. These ground and nourish you and prepare you for the situations where you may not feel as welcome, lowering the threshold of how much mental energy you have to spend to protect yourself.* ▮▮

Schools Set Up for Today's Students

Many colleges are still set up for a so-called "traditional student": a student who is 18–21 years old, white, middle-class, studying full-time, living on or near campus, and financially dependent on their parents. The reality is very different. The Lumina Foundation's Studying Students research found that 37 percent are 25 or older, 64 percent work during college (40 percent full-time), and 49 percent are financially independent.[5] Students of color may face additional obstacles to building community, finding support, and more. Colleges need to be set up for today's students to succeed.

Setting Yourself Up to Succeed

While students of color are a very diverse group and every college is different, there are lots of things you as a student of color can do to set yourself up to succeed. Go to an inclusive college or university. Find people, places, and programs where you see yourself. Manage your code switching and spend time not only with people different from you but also with others who share aspects of your identity. Seek help as you deal with race-related stress. Above all, build relationships that support you and help you feel a sense of belonging.

Tip 96. Look for an inclusive college or university.

Just as colleges vary by size, setting, type, and focus, they also vary in their progress in admitting, welcoming, including, and supporting students of color. Some are still stuck in the "access" mindset that admission and opportunity are enough. Others have progressed to a "success" mindset, where they understand the real diversity of students today and have redesigned their policies, programs, and more to provide support.

There are lots of clues to a school's inclusiveness that you can look for as part of your college search so that this isn't an extra burden for you and to improve your experience later. Beyond the basics of looking up a college on ratings and review sites and making the most of the admissions tour (see Tip 7), you can

- Look for an office of diversity, equity, and inclusion (or similar) that has made and delivered on commitments and has active programming and initiatives.

- Look up the racial and ethnic breakdown of the faculty and of the student body and the designation of the school; for instance, is it a federally designated MSI (minority-serving institution) or is it a PWI (predominately white institution)?[6]

- Research the diversity of its degree programs and curricula to see that it reflects a commitment to diversity, equity, and inclusion rather than, for example, recently cutting its African American Studies program.[7]

- Check out whether the events, clubs, and social/academic student organizations reflect racial and ethnic diversity, such as an Asian Pacific American Law Student Association, Black Business Student Association, or Society of Hispanic Engineers.

- Research (and tour) the spaces focused on students of color. Are they in basements or isolated at the edge of campus, or are they in great spaces near other groups?

Tip 97. Explore campus cultural/multicultural centers.

Colleges and universities bring together their people and support services into "centers" or "offices" to make them easier to find – on campus and online.

Cultural and/or multicultural centers can be great places to find people with shared experience, attend events, get involved, or answer your question (or direct you where you can get answers). These centers are also places you can be yourself and express yourself.

One of the things that makes these centers vibrant, valued places is that what's happening in them is determined by their community. This means you can contribute to that! You know what the needs and opportunities are so you may have an idea for an event or program – and you may know the right people on or off campus to work on this with. The space has value, but the people you meet and the organizations you join as a result have even more.

> ❚❚ *No campus is perfect at DEI. Schools have statements. They are trying to make changes. But for a lot of students, we don't feel like that's enough. You feel the most at home in a student organization that shares your race and ethnicity, like the Black Student Alliance. There is a different level of trust and comfort when you're with those students rather than an institutional center.* ❚❚

Other spaces can be particularly valuable to find community, for example, a student success center on campus with resources such as tutoring, writing and statistics help, or communications/presentation support. Connecting with teaching assistants can help too, as they are more approachable and are more likely to share your race or ethnicity.

Tip 98. Find people, places, and programs where you see yourself.

While being with people different from you (see Tip 45) is critical to your success in college, being somewhere you can be the real you (see Tip 48) and feel like you belong (see Tip 39) and feel comfortable are just as important. Find people, places, and programs where you see (and be) yourself.

> ▌▌ *Intersectionality makes it harder to see where and how you belong – where do I fit in? Feel comfortable that you will find people. You will join groups of people who understand you. It's good to be with students who are different from you, but it's also important to be understood. For me, it's my scholarship group, and since we're all first-gens, we all have the same goal: to graduate.* ▌▌

On finding programs – whether an academic program or co-curricular one like a club, internship, or event – one student of color I talked to mentioned: "It's frustrating when you don't see yourself reflected in your own education. Schools need to change, but you can seek out courses that you see yourself in. I decided to minor in social justice, and that gave me a chance to explore things I was interested in that I wasn't getting in my school, in my major."

On finding places, look for spaces where you see yourself reflected in the symbols, artwork, and names. Where the materials and sizes of spaces are comfortable. Where the location and quality of the space is on par with its importance. Where you see yourself in the other students, professors, and staff there. If these are lacking, do a space equity audit (see Tip 62) and advocate for change. Research has shown that residence halls are a particularly important place to find community.[8]

One student of color I talked to observed that:

> ▌▌ *[Colleges] offer spaces that help students express themselves. Where can you go to talk about it when you are having a hard time in classes? It might be someone's office, a center, or a club's space.* ▌▌

Tip 99. Manage your code-switching.

Changing the way you act and express yourself based on the race and ethnicity of those around you – code-switching – can be very taxing emotionally and detrimental to mental health.[9] It can also mean you're not fully present, and it can create additional anxiety over what people think about you. This came up in so many of the interviews I conducted that I thought it was important to share the advice and research folks pointed me to.

In a 2019 study, 48 percent of Black students and 42 percent of Hispanic students say they feel the need to code-switch compared to 34 percent of white students.[10] Yet, students who learn to code-switch fit in and get ahead.[11] It's also one reason people of color are much less interested in returning to work in an office following the COVID pandemic; a recent student found that Black men were half as likely as white men to want to return to working in an office full-time.[12]

> ▌▌ *Code-switching for students of color – even between parents and school – creates a lot of stress. You have to do so much work to blend in, but it's what makes you successful. You look around and see the most successful people learned to navigate different networks. So, it's taxing, but don't isolate yourself. Have your identity but join something that exposes you to other people.* ▌▌

To manage the toll of code switching, try to minimize it by picking your spots – what a *Harvard Business Review* report calls "strategic code-switching,"[13] and be sure you are spending enough time in places and with people where you don't feel like you have to code-switch, inclusive environments where people are aware of and checking their biases and you have allies.

> ▌▌ *When joining a group, get information about the people and how they work together as a team. You have agency to ask if that team is the best fit for you. If there's a red flag or a sense that you'd have to kind of fake it, then that's not the team or place for you. There are other opportunities out there. It's okay to say "no."* ▌▌

Tip 100. See how difference comes from context.

"Difference education" is an educational approach for students to learn that differences among people are based on their context – situations, backgrounds, and lived experience – not characteristics people are born with and can't change.

By reading and listening to stories that illustrate this, you can see your background not as something less than but rather as a strength, something that helps you fit into the community and empowers you to find your own path. Being with other students of color (and students who share other aspects of your identity, perhaps as a first-gen student or veteran) also empowers you to spend time with people different from you.

Race is such a complex and sensitive topic and many big, structural changes are needed to make higher education equitable. Small things can make a difference too; for instance, one research project showed that underrepresented racial minority students reading a multicultural diversity statement had higher grades two years later compared with those students who read a "colorblind" statement.[14]

Research has demonstrated that this approach could help disadvantaged students, reducing the achievement gap associated with social class by 63 percent. It also showed that students who read the multicultural statement were more comfortable talking about their different backgrounds and their impacts.[15]

I've left home. I'm in a new state. I'm around a different mix of people than I'm used to. I don't know where I fit in. The process of feeling like you belong takes time. You have to have patience with yourself. I don't think anyone who enters a new space immediately feels like they belong. It's okay.

Tip 101. Seek help as you deal with the stress of racism.

Students of color often bear extra burdens in college because of their race. This isn't fair and it's not okay, but there is help. You may experience everything from the "burden of representation" if you are the only person of color in a group to biased treatment by campus police to discrimination when you didn't get that position to racism when a slur is said or scrawled on a wall. Events beyond the campus take a toll as well.

During the pandemic, the United Negro College Fund (UNCF) conducted a national survey, and one student responded: "I'm tired, frustrated, and upset. COVID-19 [is] out here killing us and so is the police and I'm tired. I never felt like I needed more therapy in my life."[16]

These extra burdens are amplified as students of color are often less likely to seek help.[17] Students of color may feel more overwhelmed at college but keep their concerns to themselves. In a study of more than forty thousand college students at sixty schools, 23 percent of Asian-American students, 26 percent of Black students, and 33 percent of Latino students with mental health challenges sought counseling versus 46 percent of white students.

To deal with these extra burdens, take advantage of the counseling offered at your college. They are so busy, you might as well book an appointment even before you need it so you can go there when you do. Beyond counseling, seek out other forms of support from friends, a student organization, at a center, or through an outlet where you can channel how you feel into action.

Many students of color take on activism for what they believe in, and that can be a positive outlet for expressing yourself and being with others, but you should be aware that it's taxing as well (more on balancing that in Tip 93 and on self-care in Tip 95).

Tip 102. Build your network before you need it.

College is a team sport. To succeed, you need a network of people to support and challenge you so that you can learn, grow, and belong. Along the way, you'll face challenges – everyone does.

The important thing is to build your network – a big part of your "social capital" – before you need it. You don't want to be in the middle of a crisis and try to figure out who to turn to for help. One expert I talked to gave this as an example: "How will you feel, what will you do, and who will you go to if a professor is discussing a Black author's memoir and drops the N-word in class?"

You have to find people and look for opportunities to get involved and feel like you are part of a community, like you belong on campus, that you are not alone.

Building your network starts even before you enter college with the encouragement and advice of teachers, counselors, and family members.[17] It continues into college and happens by pulling together the other advice in this chapter and elsewhere in the book, including the following:

- Get involved, through a club, campus job, student service center, or the cultural and/or multicultural spaces (more on this in Tip 39).

- Seek out peers, resident advisors (RAs), professors, staff, and administrators and build a trusted relationship so you can go to them for advice and support (more on this in Tip 41).

- Be proactive in reaching out for mental health support, even booking an appointment before you might need it (More on this in Tip 36).

I put myself out there to meet new people and talked to them about what I was going through. Now we study together for exams, work on homework, and have a good time when we're not in class. Having a good support system is super helpful.

As you build your network, look for the characteristics that researchers found to be most helpful: people who you have something in common with, who can provide holistic support, who can humanize the college experience, and who have proactive philosophies.[18]

Reflection Activity: Students of Color

To make the most of this section, you need to reflect on what you've read, commit to some tips to try, and plan to apply them by thinking about what you'll do if you get stuck or have a problem – what's called an "if-then plan."

From what you just read, what might you want to try?

- Look for an inclusive college or university.
- Explore campus cultural/multicultural centers.
- Find people, places, and programs where you see yourself.
- Manage your code-switching.
- See how difference come from context.
- Seek help as you deal with the stress of racism.
- Build your network before you need it.

IF: **What might be challenging about using these tips?**

_____

_____

_____

_____

THEN: **What will you do to overcome these challenges?**

_____

_____

_____

_____

START: **What's one thing you can do right now?**

_____

_____

References

1. "Characteristics of Postsecondary Students," National Center for Education Statistics, accessed September 30, 2021, https://nces.ed.gov/programs/coe/indicator/csb?tid=74.

2. "Andrés Castro Samayoa," Faculty Directory, Boston College, n.d., https://www.bc.edu/bc-web/schools/lynch-school/faculty-research/faculty-directory/andres-castro-samayoa.html.

3. Rutgers Center for Minority Serving Institutions (website), accessed September 30, 2021, https://cmsi.gse.rutgers.edu/.

4. Center for the Study of HBCUs, Virginia Union University (website), accessed September 30, 2021, https://center4hbcu.vuu.edu/.

5. "Today's Student," *Lumina Foundation* (blog), accessed September 29, 2021, https://www.luminafoundation.org/campaign/todays-student/.

6. "The Most Ethnically Diverse National Universities in America," accessed September 30, 2021, https://www.usnews.com/best-colleges/rankings/national-universities/campus-ethnic-diversity.

7. Dawn Rhodes, "Black Studies Struggle at State Universities under Current Fiscal Climate," *Chicago Tribune*, September 6, 2016, https://www.chicagotribune.com/news/breaking/ct-african-american-studies-college-major-met-20160905-story.html.

8. Michelle Boettcher et al., "The Cultivation of Support Networks by Students of Color in a Residence Hall Setting at a Predominantly White Institution," *Journal of College and University Student Housing*, 45 no. 3 (2019): 30–46, https://eric.ed.gov/?id=EJ1220516.

9. "The Mental Health Cost of Code-Switching on Campus," *Teen Vogue*, September 11, 2019, https://www.teenvogue.com/story/the-mental-health-cost-of-code-switching-on-campus.

10. Amina Dunn, "Younger, College-Educated Black Americans Are Most Likely to Feel Need to 'Code-Switch,'" *Pew Research Center* (blog), accessed September 24, 2019, https://www.pewresearch.org/fact-tank/2019/09/24/younger-college-educated-black-americans-are-most-likely-to-feel-need-to-code-switch/.

11. Jennifer Guerra, "Teaching Students How to Switch between Black English and Standard English Can Help Them Get Ahead," State of Opportunity, Michigan Radio, July 16, 2014, https://stateofopportunity.michiganradio.org/education/2014-07-16/teaching-students-how-to-switch-between-black-english-and-standard-english-can-help-them-get-ahead.

12. Angelica Puzio, "Who Wants to Return to the Office?" FiveThirtyEight, August 11, 2021, https://fivethirtyeight.com/features/why-post-pandemic-offices-could-be-whiter-and-more-male/

13. Courtney L. McCluney et al., "The Costs of Code-Switching," *Harvard Business Review*, November 15, 2019, https://hbr.org/2019/11/the-costs-of-codeswitching.

14. Hannah Birnbaum et al., "A Diversity Ideology Intervention: Multiculturalism Reduces the Racial Achievement Gap," *Social Psychological and Personality Science*, July 23, 2020, https://doi.org/10.1177/1948550620938227.

15. Sarah S. M. Townsend, Nicole M. Stephens, and MarYam G. Hamedani, "Difference-Education Improves First-Generation Students' Grades throughout College and Increases Comfort with Social Group Difference," *Personality and Social Psychology Bulletin* 47, no. 10 (October 2021): 1510–19, https://doi.org/10.1177/0146167220982909.

16. "Student Pulse Survey: COVID-19 Impact on Fall 2020 Educational Plans," United Negro College Fund, July 2020, https://uncf.org/wp-content/uploads/UNCF-Student-Pulse-Survey-Results_Final.pdf.

17. Sarah Ketchen Lipson et al., "Mental Health Disparities among College Students of Color," *Journal of Adolescent Health* 63, no. 3 (September 2018): 348–56, https://doi.org/10.1016/j.jadohealth.2018.04.014.

18. Raquel L. Farmer-Hinton, "Social Capital and College Planning: Students of Color Using School Networks for Support and Guidance," *Education and Urban Society* 41, no. 1 (November 2008): 127–57, https://doi.org/10.1177/0013124508321373.

19. Samuel D. Museus and Kathleen M. Neville, "Delineating the Ways that Key Institutional Agents Provide Racial Minority Students with Access to Social Capital in College," *Journal of College Student Development* 53, no. 3 (2012): 436452, doi:10.1353/csd.2012.0042.

14

International Students

There are now more than a million international students studying in the US, representing a five-fold increase over the past twenty years. The enrollment of these international students is uneven by institution and major, with 40 percent of them enrolled in business programs. For this chapter, I spoke with David Austell, the director of the International Students and Scholars Office at Columbia University,[1] and I really appreciate his insights. He captured the international experience so well:

> *College is new for everyone. International students also have to deal with separation from their family, adjusting to new food and customs, and the procedures and anxiety of immigration.*

Adjusting to Being in the US

Going to college is an adjustment. You will be adjusting to a new culture, food, laws, health care, and insurance system while also dealing with additional rules regarding visas for studying, for work afterwards, or internships in between. There will be new terminology (like what does "hooking up" mean?) and new customs (like making eye contact). There are new milestones and terminology (like what's "convocation"?). Stereotypes and discrimination may also be a challenge. Beyond all this, there is uncertainty about immigration, travel, and other policies.

Adjusting to US College and Universities

The US higher education system is also an adjustment for many; other cultures may be less learner-centered with more focus on the teacher. They may not value a broad education in the liberal arts with a focus on how to think critically, be creative, and communicate rather than a specialized professional degree program directly tied to a career. As an international student, you not only need specific support services to make these adjustments, but you have specific space needs as well. This might include specific food, ablution rooms, or prayer spaces.

The good news is that international students generally have quite a positive experience, rating most aspects of their experience above the national average in the surveys I've done: campus spaces, teamwork, solving real-world problems, preparing for a future career and exploring internship options, feeling inspired, and knowing where to get help are all rated above average by international students.

Tip 103. Learn how US colleges and universities are set up.

As you prepare to study in the US, it's helpful to understand how colleges and universities are set up – and how that might vary from what you're familiar with in your home country.

Some of the key ways colleges are structured include the differences between public and private institutions, the admissions process, how to enroll and register, important rules and policies like plagiarism, what the graduation requirements are, what support services are available like advising and healthcare, and what it costs in terms of tuition, fees, and other expenses.

Beyond the campus adjustments, the career development process can also be a surprise and adjustment. You might face fewer career opportunities if employer interest/support is lacking; you will need to actively market yourself to employers, and this may be a culture shock; finally, language skills may be a barrier.

Admissions staff will often visit different countries to present information sessions on what things will be like. Another great resource is the Institute of International Education's eBook *Preparing to Study in the USA: 15 Things Every International Student Should Know*,[2] and you can also contact the international students office at the colleges or universities you are considering. Another resource is the National Association of Student Affairs Professionals (NAFSA) guide titled "US Classroom Culture."

Tip 104. Gather facts, instructions, insights, and support.

You need the right information to get the most out of college as an international student.

The American Council on Education proposed a new compact for international students[3] to ensure you feel included and are successful. It outlines four critical kinds of information you need to succeed:

- Facts, lists, rules, and procedures to serve as points of reference on policies and processes you need to know.

- Instructions as to what to do with the facts, lists, and rules, such as whom to contact with a question or to clarify a policy.

- Insights on culture to help international students (and domestic students) understand differences and similarities so you can move beyond feeling welcomed and included to really having voice and participating fully in student life.

- Sources of support for administrative questions (e.g., which form to fill out), academic questions (e.g., which course to take), and social questions (e.g., how to find community).

▟▟ *Another resource that international students can get directly from their home countries is seminars! College seminars are flooded with college reps who are well experienced and more than happy to answer any questions you have. Not only do these seminars help students know more about their prospective schools, they are also informative about what the students should expect when studying in a foreign country.* ▛▛

Tip 105. Go to the international students center.

Colleges and universities bring together their people and support services into "centers" or "offices" to make them easier to find – on campus and online.

Use the international students center or office as your go-to place online and on campus to answer your question or advise on where to get answers. They will have expert advice on highly technical matters such as visas and are also more likely to have staff with the intercultural competence to understand and assist you. The international center is so important that when it's not working, this is one the top reasons international students give for leaving their university, specifically a "lack of assistance" and "feelings of discrimination."[4]

Your international center can also connect you to other resources and communities. It will run lots of events and workshops with other parts of your college that are worth checking out. It will also have information about different international student associations, such as the Chinese Students and Scholars Association (CSSA).

▐▐ You have to find the international center and be friends with the people who work there. This is your go-to place. Involvement. Finances. Transportation. Housing. They help you get the hang of things. You learn that you are not alone. There are other international students in the same boat. ▐▐

Tip 106. Find the campus spaces that meet your needs.

Every campus is a network of spaces that are general and specific, with different sizes, shapes, locations, and vibes. Seek the spaces that meet your functional, social, cultural, and religious needs.

The international students center, clubs, professors, and friends can all be great sources of what to be on the lookout for around campus:

- Housing for living-learning communities that can be organized on an international theme or by an area you're interested in.
- Dining halls and other food options that meet your cultural and dietary needs (and talk to the director/chef about your needs).
- Spaces for clubs tied to your interests and community, which might be dedicated spaces in the student union or shared across campus.
- Ablution and prayer spaces that support your religious practices.
- Spaces whose proportions, materials, color palette, artwork, symbols, and iconography resonate with you.

> *It was hard because I left all my friends and family behind, but I took it as an opportunity to meet new people.*

Tip 107. Talk about how you are doing and feeling.

You don't have to deal with being separated from your family or the stress and anxiety of adjusting to college on your own.

Talk to a friend, advisor, or staff member at the international students center or office about how you are doing and what you are feeling. This gets you in the habit of sharing. Once you do that, people have a better sense of how they can help if you need it.

Research in the Journal of American College Health[5] has found that international students are only about half as likely as domestic students to seek mental health counseling. Getting in the habit of sharing can make mental health support a normal thing to do, and it's important to remember that counseling is something you control, something that doesn't affect your immigration status, and is confidential (including from your parents).

> ▌▌ *Sharing my mental health issues and having someone to confide in is not something we do in my country. Here there are a lot of resources and you don't have to feel like you're being discriminated against or stigmatized. Spending time with people different from me helped me get comfortable with this. People asking me if I'm okay opened me up to this.* ▌▌

Tip 108. Build a college and career network.

As an international student, you're probably arriving in the US with fewer connections to the people and places where you're studying than domestic students (and may experience more homesickness or loneliness).

It's critical that you build a network of connections so that you have the support and community you need to make the most of college as well as your career. This community should include international students and domestic students, so you surround yourself with people who can help you learn and grow, that you can help as well.

The ways to build a network and find community include the following:

- Going to the international student center for advice and to attend events and programs

- Joining a living-learning community organized around an interest or an identity

- Participating in clubs or other student organizations based on your areas of interest, including specific mentoring programs

- Seeking out coursework that has an international or multicultural theme where you're more likely to run into folks with shared interests and experience

- Looking for meals as a way to connect with people, as well as offering ideas and recipes from your home country and trying those of others

- Using your professors as a bridge; they will have recommendations for clubs, courses, and spaces around campus

Tip 109. Prepare for cultural differences in your classes.

Going to school at a college or university in the US (or an American school abroad) will include practices that may be new to you and different from the culture in your home country. Three big adjustments to be ready for:

- You'll be expected to respond to – and question – your professors, not just listen. Come to class with a few key points you want to make and a few questions you want to ask.

- You'll be expected to document the sources of your work to show what you've referenced, and you will have to build upon what you reference and make it your own rather than plagiarize or copy it.

- You'll be expected to work together with other students in groups. To do this, you'll need to collaborate – not compete – and so share information freely and create a presentation, paper, poster, or report together. Check out Tip 24 on group work for suggestions. Your school's communication center can also help with tips.

In my home country, teachers didn't hold office hours. There was no tutoring. Here, your professors are here to help you and can even accommodate you if you have a class conflict with their office hours. Tutoring is a great resource that I didn't realize was free at first.

Tip 110. Capitalize on the safer space college provides.

When you walk into the dining hall, you may see students seated separately according to country or culture. Longstanding conflicts or differences between your home country and those of other international students can divide students.

Rather than continue to reinforce those divides, you can take advantage of your college experience to have conversations with other students or professors that you can't have at home.

College provides a safer space for you to learn about, meet, and talk with students from other countries and cultures, whether you are in the classroom,[6] at an activity or event,[7] or in the multicultural center or other cultural space.[8]

> *There are international students who are shy to speak out due to language barriers. You have to do it anyway. Speak up to a lot of people. Asking professors questions in class was not a part of my culture, which was more about self study. If you don't do it, nobody is going to do it for you. There's nothing to lose if you are already at a disadvantage. You don't have to be so conscious of who you are – colleges are big places.*

Reflection Activity: International Students

To make the most of this section, you need to reflect on what you've read, commit to some tips to try, and plan to apply them by thinking about what you'll do if you get stuck or have a problem — what's called an "if-then plan."

From what you just read, what might you want to try?

- Learn how US colleges and universities are set up.
- Gather facts, instructions, insights, and support.
- Go to the international students center
- Find the campus spaces that meet your needs.
- Talk about how you are doing and feeling.
- Build a college and career network.
- Prepare for cultural differences in your classes.
- Capitalize on the safer space college provides.

IF: **What might be challenging about using these tips?**

_____

_____

_____

_____

THEN: **What will you do to overcome these challenges?**

_____

_____

_____

_____

START: **What's one thing you can do right now?**

_____

_____

References

1. International Students & Scholars Office, Columbia University in the City of New York (website), accessed September 30, 2021, https://isso.columbia.edu/.

2. "Preparing to Study in the USA: 15 Things Every International Student Should Know," IIE, accessed September 30, 2021, https://www.iie.org:443/en/Research-and-Insights/Publications/Preparing-to-Study-in-the-USA.

3. "New ACE Report Outlines Strategies for Supporting International Students Throughout Lifecycle," American Council on Education, February 12, 2021, https://www.acenet.edu/News-Room/Pages/ACE-Report-Outlines-Strategies-for-Supporting-International-Students.aspx.

4. Clayton Smith, "International Student Success," Strategic *Enrollment Management Quarterly* 4, no 2 (2016): 61–73.

5. Jenny Hyun et al., "Mental Health Need, Awareness, and Use of Counseling Services Among International Graduate Students," *Journal of American College Health* 56, no. 2 (2007): 109–18, https://doi.org/10.3200/JACH.56.2.109-118.

6. Alicia Fedelina Chavez, "Islands of Empowerment: Facilitating Multicultural Learning Communities in College," *International Journal of Teaching and Learning in Higher Education* 19, no. 3 (2007): 274–88.

7. Chun-Mei Zhao, "Achieving Multicultural Competence: Student Participation in College Activities and Its Impact on Multicultural Learning David Cheng," vol. 21 (45th Annual AIR Forum-Enhancing knowledge, Expanding networks, Citeseer, 2005), https://citeseerx.ist.psu.edu/viewdoc/download?doi=10.1.1.561.8402&rep=rep1&type=pdf.

8. "All Campuses Need Cultural Spaces," *Diverse: Issues In Higher Education*, August 25, 2015, https://www.diverseeducation.com/opinion/article/15097063/all-campuses-need-cultural-spaces.

15

Veteran Students

There were more than 650,000 veterans enrolled in college as of 2018.[1] For this chapter, I spoke with Stephen Ross, the director of Virginia Commonwealth University's Military Student Services.[2] I am grateful for his perspective and contributions. One thing he said summed up the student veteran experience well:

> **■■** *Most veteran students excel if they adapt well. They have to engage beyond the classroom and move from a mindset of compliance to commitment.* **■■**

Life in the military can be quite different from college. You have more choice and control over where, how, and what you spend your time on. You've had life experiences, such as losing a friend on the battlefield, that your classmates may not have. Your years in the military mean you're older than many of your peers and you have other responsibilities to your job and family.

Adjusting to College as a Veteran

Going to college will be an adjustment as you figure out how to adapt. You'll have to decide how much of the structure and routine from the military career to forward into college. Your new learning environment may be less technical and the culture may be less top-down. You'll have to get involved beyond your classes to succeed. You'll have to learn and work with students who are different from you. If you find support and community and are open to difference, you'll do well.

Using Your Service as a Strength

The good news is that your military service is an asset. A 2020 study of veterans identified veterans' students strengths as experience with diverse places and people; leadership skills, including mentoring and delegation; and drive, including discipline, work ethic, and focus.[3] Veteran students are more likely to graduate compared to other adult learners[4] who have not served, and veterans do so with higher average GPAs[5] than traditional students. You've learned the benefits of discipline and hard work. You have additional life experience and perspective. You've shed many of the bad habits from high school, like procrastinating.

Tip 111. Look for a veteran-friendly college or university.

Nearly all colleges and universities say they welcome and support veteran students. In reality, only certain institutions have seamless support services and thriving communities. Finding one will increase your chance of success.

One interviewee in a study of veteran student identity noted, "You can see a lot of vets on campus; you know, the way that they walk, the way that they handle themselves, the way that they speak, and you get to talking to these people and it's information that gets shared back and forth, just a mutual understanding."[7]

To find a college or university that is focused on veteran student success, look for

- Transition programs and classes, which may be called "Boots to Books" or "Combat to Classroom" or similar[8]

- "Green Zone" programs that educate faculty and staff so they can lend an informed and sympathetic ear

- An active Student Veterans of America (SVA) chapter on campus

- A center or office of veteran students to centralize people and services that can help

- Participation in the US Department of Veterans Affairs Yellow Ribbon Program,[9] where they waive some or all of the tuition and fees that exceed the maximum GI Bill benefits

- Listed as veteran friendly in ranking or review sites like USNews or bestcolleges.com or niche.com

Once you find a veteran-friendly college or university, be sure to take advantage of these resources; talk to a professor who's served, go to SVA events, and stop by the veteran student center.

> *You go from an environment where everyone is part of a team and everyone belongs to one where everyone is different than you from age perspective and you are wondering, is this place meant for you...? There was definitely an adjustment: where do I fit in? Where do I belong? It's weird being older. Being a veteran, you sometimes have a gut feeling that maybe not everyone likes that.*

Tip 112. Go to the veterans center.

Colleges and universities bring together their people and support services into "centers" or "offices" to make them easier to find – on campus and online.

Your school's veterans center can help you simplify the complexity of being a student veteran. It may be about explaining how GI Bill benefits work for you, your children, and your spouse – or connecting you with the financial aid office to do so. It may be about understanding how insurance works or how to access mental health services. It may be about learning skills to help you adjust. In addition to the local resources offered at your college or university, the center can also tell you about national organizations like the Student Veterans of America[8] and the VA's VetSuccess on Campus program.[10]

A veteran's center is not only a place for finding resources and information but community as well. It's a place to connect with other vets for workshops, meals, and other events so you can be part of a community, feel a sense of belonging, and know you're not in it alone.

> A veterans center is a big resource for incoming vets. There's a lot of weird stuff you have to navigate that people don't think about, like you get your tuition bill and it's really high and you wonder and worry about paying for it. They'll help you understand you have to wait for GI bill benefits to kick in. Or tell you that you don't have to sign up for and pay for student health insurance if you are covered by the VA.

Tip 113. Decide how much of the structure and routine from the military you want to carry forward into college.

Veteran student success expert Stephen Ross notes that veteran students have learned the benefits of structure, discipline, and hard work during their time in the military – and gotten rid of some of the bad habits from high school that can get in the way of success.

One interviewee in a study of veteran student identity noted: "I kinda feel that coming out of [the military] and having the discipline and the sense of duty and this want to succeed that was kind of ingrained in me; it helped me transition into that program and make sure I could actually handle the workload that was involved with that."[11]

Going to college will be an adjustment that comes with choices about how, where, and on what you spend your time. To use your military experience as an asset, think about what routines and habits you can apply to college life when deciding about what your day looks like, including exercise, study, meals, and more.

One way to think about the transition is using the recently developed Veterans Adjustment to College scale.[12] There are also national resources and support services that can help with this transition, such as the VA's Veterans Integration to Academic Leadership Program.[13]

The military is super structured. In a lot of ways college is too. Classes are a certain time. Homework is due. You have deadlines. In a lot of ways, I feel like I don't have as much independence as I used to. I used to work 9–5 in the military and the evenings were my own. Now my time isn't all my time anymore.

Tip 114. Engage in college life – don't just go to class and back home.

Veteran students are less likely to attend events, join clubs, or participate in other aspects of college life outside of their classes.

This is often for good reason, as you may have additional financial or family responsibilities. However, even a few activities can make a big difference in connecting you to people and experiences that will help you get more out of college.

In one research report[14] by the US Veterans Affairs Department, a veteran student noted: "I'm from Atlanta, where the politics are 180 degrees different from UC-Berkeley and the township of Berkeley.... And so I've become a better person. I've challenged some of my own personal beliefs by coming here. I definitely have gotten way more patient with some of these kids when hearing some of the stuff that comes out of their mouths. I've also learned a lot from these kids because they're smart. The professors are amazing."

A great place to start are events organized through your veteran student office/center, as these are tailored to you and you'll have a lot in common with other attendees. As you get more comfortable, expand to other activities and student organizations based on your major, your interests, and your friends' recommendations. Getting involved will also mean spending time with people different from you (more on this in Tip 45).

I wanted to throw myself into as much of a traditional college experience as I could. For some people, living off-campus works for them. For me, that started with living on campus so I had a community outside of my veteran group. Knowing those people helped me feel more comfortable to try other things at the university. Feeling a little more welcomed and accepted than I would have had I just stuck with the people I knew, with the people who are exactly like me.

Tip 115. Look for opportunities for team learning.

So much of your experience in the military involved working in teams. Going to college and doing a lot of individual work can be a shock.

Research has found that veteran students found cohort model learning much more compatible and comfortable. It increased their motivation by improving their self-confidence and competence.

A cohort/team may be organized through a class at your college or be through a cohort-based program like the Posse Foundation's Veterans Program.[15] One Posse program participant noted: "When you have people with similar experiences as you... it helps you feel at ease." Another participant noted: "My Posse is a support system – nine other women and my mentor on campus who I know will always be there for me.... I don't have to navigate college alone. To me that's the best feeling ever." [16]

To lessen the shock and build on your skills and strengths, look for opportunities to learn as part of a cohort of students that takes the same classes and to have a consistent group of students to work on projects with.

> ❚❚ Most of my classes have been group based, especially in
> business. Most majors are incorporating leadership and teamwork
> in some way. There aren't as many opportunities to learn about this
> outside of classes. Classes work better because the stakes are higher
> than a club. I use these projects to learn about myself, what kind of
> leader I am, and how to react in different situations. ❚❚

Tip 116. Build the network you need for civilian success the rest of your life.

Engaging in college life is difficult when so many students are younger than you, haven't had the same experiences you have, and don't have the family/financial obligations that you may have. However, networking with other students will not only give you a supportive community to help you thrive in college, but create a network for the rest of your life, personally and professionally.

> *Being engaged in clubs has been helpful for networking and job stuff, but it's also been great to do things I won't be able to do later when I'm working, like performing. Besides meeting a lot of people with similar interests, it just makes everything else more fun. It's time to decompress and step away.*

To build your network, tap your college's career services center, get on veteran's email newsletters, sign up for text lists for topics of interest, attend veteran-focused events where it will be easier to make a connection, and ask to visit or shadow an alum. Throughout, think about not only what you want to get out of this involvement but what you have to contribute.

> *Don't expect clubs to give you connections. Think about what you can offer them. Putting yourself out there is about being helpful, and then connections naturally come rather than expecting "community" to come to you.*

Reflection Activity: Veteran Students

To make the most of this section, you need to reflect on what you've read, commit to some tips to try, and plan to apply them by thinking about what you'll do if you get stuck or have a problem – what's called an "if-then plan."

From what you just read, what might you want to try?

- Look for a veteran-friendly college or university.
- Go to the veteran center.
- Decide how much of the structure and routine from the military you want to carry forward into college.
- Engage in college life – don't just go to class and back home.
- Look for opportunities for team learning.
- Build the network you need for civilian success the rest of your life.

IF: **What might be challenging about using these tips?**

_____

_____

_____

_____

_____

THEN: **What will you do to overcome these challenges?**

_____

_____

_____

_____

START: **What's one thing you can do right now?**

_____

_____

References

1. "Veterans in Higher Education," PNPI, November 9, 2019, https://pnpi.org/veterans-in-higher-education/.

2. "Military Student Services," Virginia Commonwealth University, accessed September 30, 2021, https://militaryservices.vcu.edu/.

3. Katie Sullivan and Kay Yoon, "Student Veterans' Strengths: Exploring Student Veterans' Perceptions of Their Strengths and How to Harness Them in Higher Education," *Journal of Continuing Higher Education* 68, no. 3 (September 2020): 164–80, https://doi.org/10.1080/07377 363.2020.1806013.

4. "New Report: Enrolling More Veterans at High-Graduation-Rate Colleges and Universities," *Ithaka S+R* (blog), January 10, 2019, https://sr.ithaka.org/blog/new-report-enrolling-more-veterans-at-high-graduation-rate-colleges-and-universities/.

5. "Veterans in Higher Education."

6. Natalie Gross, "From 'Boots to Books': How Tailored College Classes Help Vets in Transition," Reboot Camp, August 24, 2018, https://rebootcamp.militarytimes.com/news/education/2018/08/24/from-boots-to-books-how-tailored-college-classes-help-vets-in-transition/.

7. Corrine E. Hinton, "'I Just Don't Like to Have My Car Marked': Nuancing Identity Attachments and Belonging in Student Veterans," *Journal of Veterans Studies* 6, no. 3 (December 2020): 84–100, https://doi.org/10.21061/jvs.v6i3.211.

8. Student Veterans of America (website), accessed September 30, 2021, https://studentveterans. org/.

9. "Find a Yellow Ribbon School," US Department of Veterans Affairs, accessed September 30, 2021, https://www.va.gov/education/yellow-ribbon-participating-schools/.

10. "VetSuccess on Campus," US Department of Veterans Affairs, accessed September 30, 2021, https://www.benefits.va.gov/vocrehab/vsoc.asp.

11. Hinton, "'I Just Don't Like to Have My Car Marked.'"

12. Sharon Young, "Veterans Adjustment to College: Construction and Validation of a Scale," *Journal of Veterans Studies* 2 (June 2017): 13, https://doi.org/10.21061/jvs.13.

13. "VA College Toolkit: Services," accessed September 30, 2021, https://www.mentalhealth.va.gov/student-veteran/services.asp.

14. Mike Richman, "Navigating the College Experience," US Department of Veterans Affairs, October 6, 2017, https://www.research.va.gov/currents/1017-Veterans-face-challenges-in-higher-education.cfm.

15. The Posse Foundation. "The Posse Veterans Program." Accessed September 29, 2021. https://www.possefoundation.org/shaping-the-future/posse-veterans-program.

16. Edward J. Campbell, "Veteran Student Success: An Evaluation of Veteran Students' Perceptions of a Cohort Learning Model" (PhD diss., Oregon State University, 2016).

16

Transfer Students

About a third of college students transfer before earning their degree.[1] Students are finding affordable ways to access education, taking charge of their college and career, and capitalizing on easier ways to combine their credits from multiple colleges toward a degree.

For this chapter, I spoke with Randi Harris, the director of Portland State University's Transfer and Returning Student Resource Center.[2] She had great insights to share, including,

> ▟▟ You don't know what you need until you need it. We can't expect students to be aware of hundreds of resources. But we can expect them to know a few folks who can help them and point them to resources they may not know are available. ▟▟

Transferring is the New Normal

Transferring is a normal thing for you to do; don't feel weird about it. There will be even more of it in the future. But it's still hard because so much is new. Your classes, clubs, campus, and community are all new. This change can lead to "transfer shock," where your grades go down initially.

Building on Transfer Students' Strengths

The good news is that transfer students have a leg up. You are resilient. You have experience and perspective on how things work from your last college or university. Because of this, transfer students generally have a higher chance of graduating[3] and are more innovative[4] than students who don't transfer. To get those results, you need to be resourceful and your best bet is to find a go-to person who can tell you where to go.

Tip 117. Go to the Transfer Center.

Colleges and universities bring together their people and support services into "centers" or "offices" to make them easier to find – on campus and online.

Your transfer center or office will have information and staff to help you with unique issues of transfer students, including getting credit for prior learning/work, explaining transfer-specific policies and procedures, signing up to receive updates, and orienting you generally to your new environment.

The center may also provide programs and services such as advising sessions by appointment or drop-in, as well as workshops and other events. There are also often opportunities to connect with peers who've gone through what you are going through and can tell you what worked and what didn't for them.

You have to find people and look for opportunities to get involved and feel like you are part of a community, like you belong on campus, that you are not alone – so many of the people I have met happen to be transfer students, and I wasn't even looking for them. My university sends out a survey after you attend an event and they want to know if you feel like part of the community, if you have the resources you need.

(If you are looking for a school to transfer to, having a transfer center or office is a good sign that a school is transfer friendly. Look for the center as part of your search.)

Tip 118. Get credit for your prior experience.

What you get credit for from your prior classes and work experience will have a huge impact on your experience when you transfer into your new institution. By a 2017 US government estimate, transfers lose an average 43 percent of their credits.[5]

The more credit you get, the more flexibility you'll have to take the courses you want to. This can save you time and money toward graduation. It will also help you avoid the boredom and frustration of retaking something that's similar to a course you already completed.

Look at your college or university's transfer agreements with other schools and their credit transfer policy in detail. Look specifically to see if there's a way to petition for more credits than they gave you initially, as well as if they can give credit for prior related work experience you have. There are also scholarships available specifically for transfer students, so that's worth researching as well.

Tip 119. Reflect on what expectations to let go of from your prior institution.

As you learn about and get oriented to your new college or university, you'll be looking at it through the lens of your previous school. This has pros and cons.

You have a leg up, knowing how colleges work and how you need to work, but you also have a bunch of expectations that may not be met whenever your new school is different.

Try to think about what's different and what to let go of. Consider things like the policies and procedures, the technology for registering for classes and taking them, what spaces are available and how they are used, and how clubs and other student organizations work.

> *Being a transfer student is definitely a process of adapting, especially going from a community college to a four-year college. The size, having teaching assistants, Greek Life are all different. You have to let go of a lot of what you did before. It's a learning curve. Finding your rhythm, finding your place, finding your people. It takes time. If you have the right mindset about learning and growing, it will work out.*

Tip 120. Prepare for and prevent "transfer shock."

Transfer students often have similar GPAs[6] and are more likely to graduate[7] than those who start in their first year, especially if you get an associate's degree first. But many transfer students experience a slight dip in their grades in the first semester or two.

To keep this from happening to you, get the support you need in advance. This way, if you get a low grade on a test or experience other setbacks, you know where to go to get help making adjustments right away.

Getting the support in place means acting on many of the other tips in this section, such as using the transfer center. You can also talk to a friend or advisor and do a "premortem," where you talk about all the things that could go wrong and what you'll do to either prevent them or deal with them.[8]

Tip 121. Help other transfer students.

As you learn the ropes, you can help other transfer students adapt, survive, and thrive in college. This will not only be a chance to give back but to learn more about yourself and find community in the process.

Being a "transfer agent" or "transfer champion" means understanding other students' needs and guiding them toward success so they can benefit from your experience. It will also help dispel common myths like transfer students' "getting" college already and not needing help. One transfer student put it simply: "Be the person you wish you had when you were younger."

There are lots of ways to get involved, such as conducting the orientation for transfer students, telling your story in panel discussions and online, actively advising or mentoring other transfer students, or serving as an "ambassador" for your college or nationally for an organization like NISTS, the National Institute for the Study of Transfer Students.[9]

> College was a big jump, a big cost I was responsible for, but I didn't have anyone to ask about where to live or what to study. I didn't feel like my advisor helped me a lot. It was better to talk to students older than me. There are a lot of workarounds I didn't know about, for instance, requirements can double-dip. One class can count for two requirements. Now I'm helping students younger than me.

Reflection Activity: Transfer Students

To make the most of this section, you need to reflect on what you've read, commit to some tips to try, and plan to apply them by thinking about what you'll do if you get stuck or have a problem — what's called an "if-then plan."

From what you just read, what might you want to try?

- Go to the transfer center.
- Get credit for your prior experience.
- Reflect on what expectations to let go of from your prior institution.
- Prepare for and prevent "transfer shock."
- Help other transfer students.

IF: **What might be challenging about using these tips?**

_____

_____

_____

_____

_____

THEN: **What will you do to overcome these challenges?**

_____

_____

_____

_____

START: **What's one thing you can do right now?**

_____

_____

References

1. "Tracking Transfer," National Student Clearinghouse Research Center, September 23, 2021, https://nscresearchcenter.org/tracking-transfer/.

2. Transfer & Returning Student Resource Center," Portland State University," accessed September 30, 2021, https://www.pdx.edu/transfer-center/.

3. "Persistence: The Success of Students Who Transfer from Community Colleges to Selective Four-Year Institutions," Jack Kent Cooke Foundation, accessed September 30, 2021, https://www.jkcf.org/research/persistence/.

4. "Want to Hire an Innovative College Graduate? Choose a Transfer Student," EdSurge, June 2, 2021, https://www.edsurge.com/news/2021-06-02-want-to-hire-an-innovative-college-graduate-choose-a-transfer-student.

5. "Higher Education: Students Need More Information to Help Reduce Challenges in Transferring College Credits," US Government Accountability Office, August 14, 2017, https://www.gao.gov/products/gao-17-574.

6. Grace Chen, "How Well do Community College Students Perform after Transferring?" Community College Review. October 10, 2020, https://www.communitycollegereview.com/blog/how-well-do-community-college-students-perform-after-transferring.

7. "Graduate, Transfer, Graduate," accessed September 30, 2021, https://www.insidehighered.com/news/2012/11/08/high-graduation-rates-community-college-transfers.

8. Gary Klein, "Performing a Project Premortem," *Harvard Business Review*, September 2007, https://hbr.org/2007/09/performing-a-project-premortem.

9. The National Institute for the Study of Transfer Students (website), accessed September 30, 2021, https://www.nists.org.

17

Student Athletes

There are about 460,000 intercollegiate student athletes in the US. The national student surveys I've done have consistently found that student-athletes have the highest satisfaction with their college or university and the highest sense of belonging, comfort in taking risks, teamwork, personal growth, feeling supported, and many more aspects of the college experience.

Athletes' Unique Experience

Student athletes have a unique experience and expectations. Because of training, practices, and games on- and off-season, you are focused on your sport year-round. You are held accountable for your athletic and academic performance. You have less control.

For this chapter, I spoke with student athlete expert Bill Carter from Student Athlete Insights[1] and am grateful for his acumen and advice. One thing he noted about student athletes really struck me:

> *Your time is not your own. You are being told where to be. Where to eat. When to be in the weight room. That push and pull by real authority figures lends itself to a higher level of stress.*

Surviving and Thriving as a Student-Athlete

While these aspects of being a student athlete are timeless, some are changing. You can now earn money from your name, image, and likeness (NIL). You expect, and rightly so, a two-way relationship with your college or university to receive more leadership opportunities, mental health support, and career development than nonathletes. Compared to previous generations of student athletes, your parents tend to be more involved, which means you have more support but may also have more distractions and complications.

The tips in this section will help you understand the resources available to you and take advantage of them so that you too can get out of your sport what you put in, if not more.

Tip 122. Go to the student-athlete center.

Colleges and universities bring together their people and support services into "centers" or "offices" to make them easier to find – on campus and online.

Being a student athlete brings with it unique challenges and opportunities; for instance, your daily schedule might be quite different from that of nonathletes by including training and practices. Special support services such as tutoring and mentoring might be available to you as an athlete.

If your school has a student-athlete center or office, you can use it to learn about and access these services or learn about unique policies such as early registration for classes. The center can also help with how to bring together academics and athletics. It can provide associated support services such as tutoring, writing help, and academic skills coaching.[2]

One center director reflected on her job here: "I most enjoy the daily interaction with the student-athletes.... Our program helps the athletes help themselves. One of the most rewarding parts of the job is to watch them develop the necessary skills to allow them to succeed both in and out of the classroom."[3]

Tip 123. Set boundaries with your family.

Your family has probably been a big part of your success as a student-athlete to get you where you are – encouraging and advising you, shuttling you to practices and games, and watching from the stands.

In college, they need to know you still value their support, but they'll have less access and less influence and be involved in different ways.[4] Your schedule will be full, with less time to talk to and see them. You'll have more coaches, trainers, advisors, and peers that you need to pay attention to and learn from.

Talk with your parents/guardians about how it will be different. Help them understand how you need to focus on academics and athletics. Let your coaches and others do their job so your family doesn't pull you in different directions.

(See Tip 14 for more on setting expectations and boundaries with your family, and keep in mind that every family is different and expectations can vary by culture too.)

Tip 124. Look for a two-way relationship with your athletic program.

You can get a lot out of a sport by just showing up to practices and games. But you should take advantage of your school's resources to get the most out of the experience.

Be assertive in asking about and capitalizing on chances to develop your leadership skills, identify your career path, develop your network, and access mental health support (which is normal and okay to talk about!).

Find out what's available from the student-athlete center and talk to your coaches and older players. Then, attend every leadership training session, counseling session, career planning workshop, or alumni networking event you can.

In a story about connecting student-athletes with career opportunities, one student athlete reflected on being a Mayo Clinic Innovation Scholar:

> As an athlete, it not only allowed me to highlight and strengthen my team-minded work skills, but it also gave me an opportunity to step into the world of business, and see the medical world through the lens of the business, which is not something that I get to see as a science student very consistently.[5]

Tip 125. Connect directly with alumni from your program.

In addition to building knowledge and skills in college, you are also building a network. These relationships will support you the rest of your life, personally and professionally.

More than just attending the same college or university, playing the same sport (perhaps even for the same coach) creates a shared experience and strong connection between present and past student-athletes. Many athletics departments are embracing their role to measure success beyond graduation rate and include career outcomes as well.[6]

Student-athlete expert Bill Carter recommends incoming students ask their coach or recruiter how their alumni network is used for career development – what are the specific ways that student-athletes and alums are formally connected?

Two ways to make these connections are through social media and attending alumni networking events. Social media tools have made connecting easier and more accessible than ever, but tools alone won't make the connections; people and programs will.

One student athlete reflected on this:

> Former athletes know some of the skills that athletes bring to the table, like leadership and dedication, but in order to connect on a professional level, it is essential to convey how the skills demonstrated on the field apply in the office. Without concrete professional experience, it is difficult to convey these skills to employers.[7]

Tip 126. Cope with less control.

Students come to college expecting more freedom, but as a student athlete you may have less. Coaches, trainers, advisors, and others may be telling you where, when, and how you eat, sleep, exercise, and more. It can be very hard to stand up to a coach, trainer, or other authority figure – especially if you are worried about losing playing time, what they think of you, and more.

Several studies of student athletes have shown that less control can lead to more stress. Develop the skills to cope with less control by both gaining some control and changing how you react when you don't have enough.[8]

To gain control, try to carefully test boundaries to figure out what really matters and then pick your battles. Maybe that regimen, practice, or diet was really a suggestion and not a requirement?

To change how you react:

- *Know it and name it* when you feel frustrated or angry because of all the things you are being told to do.

- *Look for an upside*: your coach's rules mean fewer things you have to think about so you can focus on other things.

- *Work to cultivate an "internal locus of control"* where your drive comes from inside you, not what other people think about you and tell you. One way to measure this is through researcher Hanna Levenson's multidimensional locus of control scale[9] using a worksheet or checklist based on it.[10]

Tip 127. Benefit from your name, image, and likeness.

In what is perhaps the biggest change to college sports in a generation, student athletes are now allowed to make money by selling their name, image, and likeness (NIL). While there is not yet a federal law, nearly forty states have or will soon have their own, and the NCAA has policies in the interim.

Student-athlete expert Bill Carter recommends:

- *Understand the NCAA rules:* Some highlights include: NIL can't impact recruiting. Compensation is for work performed. NIL can't conflict with academic or team activities. Compensation cannot be "pay for play." An employee of a college/university cannot pay a student-athlete, and compensation must be fair market value. [11]

- *Develop a personal brand* that is real, human, authentic, and unique enough to stand out from nearly 500,000 other student athletes. Ask yourself: What will you be doing? Who else is doing these? How will you be different or better? Why should people believe you?

- *Use social media* to promote your personal brand and the brands you work with. Think about content aligned to your brand and consistency to build influence. Remember this is different from what you do with your friends. Aim for 1–3 posts daily on LinkedIn, Instagram, TikTok, and Twitter.

- *Be creatively entrepreneurial* to think beyond product endorsements – consider promotions like camps, clinics, private instruction, autograph signings, merchandise, and personal appearances.

Reflection Activity: Student-Athletes

To make the most of this section, you need to reflect on what you've read, commit to some tips to try, and plan to apply them by thinking about what you'll do if you get stuck or have a problem — what's called an "if-then plan."

From what you just read, what might you want to try?

- Go to the student athlete center.
- Set boundaries with your family.
- Look for a two-way relationship with your athletic program.
- Connect directly with alumni from your program.
- Cope with less control.
- Benefit from your name, image, and likeness.

IF: **What might be challenging about using these tips?**

_____

_____

_____

_____

_____

THEN: **What will you do to overcome these challenges?**

_____

_____

_____

_____

START: **What's one thing you can do right now?**

_____

_____

References

1. Student-Athlete Insights (website), accessed September 30, 2021, https://studentathleteinsights. com/.

2. Dan Tynan, "How Academic Centers Help Student-Athletes Hit Peak Performance," *EdTech*, Feburary 21, 2019, https://edtechmagazine.com/higher/article/2019/02/how-academic-centers-help-student-athletes-hit-peak-performance.

3. "Center for Student-Athlete Enhancement," Marist College, accessed September 29, 2021, https://www.marist.edu/student-life/athletics/student-athlete-enhancement.

4. Katie Lowe and Travis Dorsch, "Parents of NCAA Student-Athletes: How Are They Involved and Does It Matter?" *Athletic Director U* (blog), September 24, 2019, https://athleticdirectoru.com/articles/does-parental-involvement-matter-ncaa-student-athletes/.

5. Austin Lagesse, "Student-Athlete Career Success Stories," Bethel University Athletics, April 14, 2020, https://athletics.bethel.edu/news/2020/4/14/general-student-athlete-career-success-stories.aspx.

6. Kevin Blue and Ryan Craig, "Opinion: College Athletics Departments Do a Better Job Counseling Students than Career Offices," *The Hechinger Report*, February 5, 2019, http://hechingerreport.org/opinion-college-athletics-departments-do-better-job-counseling-students/.

7. Nic Baird, "How Student Athletes Can Build Meaningful Relationships with Alumni," Parker Dewey, March 28, 2019, https://www.parkerdewey.com/blog/student-athletes-relationships-with-alumni.

8. Shelley L. Holden et al., "Sport Locus of Control and Perceived Stress among College Student-Athletes," *International Journal of Environmental Research and Public Health* 16, no. 16 (August 2019): 2823, https://doi.org/10.3390/ijerph16162823.

9. H. Levenson, "Multidimensional Locus of Control in Psychiatric Patients," *Journal of Consulting and. Clinical Psychology* 41 (1973): 397–404.

10. Insel, Paul, and Walton Roth. "Levenson Multidimensional Locus of Control Scales: Wellness Worksheet 6." In *Core Concepts in Health*, 10th ed. McGraw-Hill, 2006. https://osf.io/h7sqj/download.

11. Michelle Hosick, "NCAA Adopts Interim Name, Image and Likeness Policy," NCAA, June 30, 2021, https://www.ncaa.org/about/resources/media-center/news/ncaa-adopts-interim-name-image-and-likeness-policy.

Conclusion

College isn't something you navigate to get through like it's an obstacle course, though it can feel like one. It's an experience you design to ensure you get the most out of college. Yes, it's part of the higher education system and like any system, it's big, daunting, and confusing. But it is also a system that provides amazing opportunities, resources, and support.

At their best, colleges can offer affordable access, inspiring classes, and support the whole student. They can do research that solves real problems for real people. They can offer people work with purpose. They can be diverse, inclusive communities that are set in remarkable places. They can help all students succeed, no matter their race, income, or background.

This book shows how to get the most out of college so you can leave better connected to a purpose and career path. Better connected to the information and knowledge you need. Better connected to the valuable skills you've built. Better connected to the communities you're a part of. Better connected the place you're in.

There are suggestions on how to achieve this on every page and a chance to reflect, apply, and commit in every section. As you finish the book – whether you went cover to cover or jumped around – you have the chance to put it all together and to pay it forward in five ways:

- *Mark it:* Go back through your sticky notes, highlights, and bookmarks to pull out the ideas that are the most relevant for you. Put these up on your wall so they are visible.

- *Map it:* As you pull out what you've learned, find the connections so you can double or triple what you get out of it. What tips are related and which can you combine?

- *Make it happen:* Put the action items into practice. Go through the reflection activities and hold yourself accountable – have you done the things you said you'd try? Talk to friends about what you want to do so they can support and check up on you.

- *Manage it:* Even with the best of intentions, hard work, and support, it may not work out. Try to manage expectations and make a plan. You can stick it out, switch programs, switch colleges, slow down to part-time, or take time off.

- ■ *Make it better:* This book is about leveling the playing field so that all students have opportunities to learn, grow, belong, and succeed, especially students with fewer resources and relationships. If you benefited from this book at all, now is your chance to help someone else:

  - Tell someone about this book and walk them through how you used it and how it helped them.

  - Become a mentor or advisor, either through a formal program at your college or just informally among friends, so you can advise and support someone.

  - Give feedback and suggestions to your college on what's working and what isn't so they can do an even better job helping tomorrow's students.

One final tip: What you do to succeed in college is what you need to do to succeed in life. Understand yourself. Build relationships. Work together. Ask questions and ask for help. Keep it up!

Acknowledgments

This book was shaped by conversations with students, advisors, and experts. Their insights, counsel, research, and references contributed greatly to *How to Get the Most Out of College*, and for that I am forever grateful.

I'd like to thank the many students who provided input and feedback on the content, structure, language, and tone of the book: Abby Anderson, Annie Phan, Ayman Siam, Austin Cox, Catherine Chattergoon, Dan Ogranovich, Derrick McDonald, Ellie Egbert, Fernando Sanchez Lopez, Genesis Rogers, Jason Xiong, Lizbeth Parra, Natalie Passov, and Sofia Melian-Morse.

I'd also like to thank the many experts in their respective fields whom I interviewed so that I could better understand and benefit from their work: Andres Castro Samayoa, Bill Carter, Carol Brandt, Chaunté White, Christine Chu, Christine Logel, David Austell, Deana Waintraub Stafford, Genny Beemyn, Janice Fournier, Jennifer Keup, Katy DeRosier, Michaelann Jundt, Randi Harris, Shawn Calhoun, Stephen T. Ross, Terrell Strayhorn, Tim Montgomery, and William Washington.

Finally, I'd like to thank my past and present colleagues and collaborators at DEGW, brightspot, and Buro Happold as well as a group of trusted advisors who provided counsel and were great thought partners on the goals, format, and concepts in the book: Ben Maddox, Bill Mayer, Cedric Howard, Craig Bida, David Clark, Dick Minturn, Enku Gelaye, Evelyn Hsieh Wong, Kathe Pelletier, John Katzman, Joseph Cevetello, Julie Dirksen, Sukhwant Jhaj, and Tom Ellett.

Bibliography

"7 Things You Should Know about the HyFlex Course Model." Accessed September 30, 2021. https://library.educause.edu/resources/2020/7/7-things-you-should-know-about-the-hyflex-course-model.

16 Personalities. "Free Personality Test." Accessed September 29, 2021. https://www.16personalities.com/.

Abilock, Debbie, Susan D. Ballard, Tasha Bergson-Michelson, Jennifer Colby, Kristin Frontichiaro, and Amy Lennex. *Creating Data Literate Students*. Ann Arbor, MI: Michigan Publishing, University of Michigan Library, 2017. http://dx.doi.org/10.3998/mpub.9873254.

"All Campuses Need Cultural Spaces," *Diverse: Issues in Higher Education,* August 25, 2015. https://www.diverseeducation.com/opinion/article/15097063/all-campuses-need-cultural-spaces.

American College Health Association. "National College Health Assessment II: Reference Group Executive Summary." Silver Spring, MD: ACHA, 2019. https://www.acha.org/documents/ncha/ncha-ii_spring_2019_us_reference_group_executive_summary.pdf.

American Council on Education. Association of American Colleges & Universities. "Strategies for Student-Parent Success at the University of Alabama," May 2014. https://www.aacu.org/campus-model/strategies-student-parent-success-university-alabama.

Baird, Nic. "How Student Athletes Can Build Meaningful Relationships with Alumni." Parker Dewey. Accessed September 29, 2021. https://www.parkerdewey.com/blog/student-athletes-relationships-with-alumni.

Bartle-Haring, Suzanne, Penny Brucker, and Ellen Hock. "The Impact of Parental Separation Anxiety on Identity Development in Late Adolescence and Early Adulthood." *Journal of Adolescent* 17 (2002): 439–50. https://doi.org/10.1177/0743558402175001.

Bellevue College Disability Resource Center. "Success Stories." Accessed September 30, 2021. https://www.bellevuecollege.edu/drc/success-stories/.

"The Best Colleges for First-Generation College Students." TheBestColleges.org, April 10, 2013. https://www.thebestcolleges.org/the-best-colleges-for-first-generation-college-students/.

Betancur, Laura, Benjamin Margolin Rottman, Elizabeth Votruba-Drzal, and Christian Schunn. "Analytical Assessment of Course Sequencing: The Case of Methodological Courses in Psychology." *Journal of Educational Psychology* 111, no. 1 (2019): 91–103. https://doi.org/10.1037/edu0000269.

Bettinger, Eric P., and Rachel B. Baker. "The Effects of Student Coaching: An Evaluation of a Randomized Experiment in Student Advising." *Educational Evaluation and Policy Analysis* 36, no. 1 (2014): 3–19.

Birnbaum, Hannah et al. "A Diversity Ideology Intervention: Multiculturalism Reduces the Racial Achievement Gap." *Social Psychological and Personality Science*, July 23, 2020. https://doi.org/10.1177/1948550620938227.

Blackstone Launchpad. "Entrepreneurship Training for Students." Accessed September 29, 2021. https://www.blackstonelaunchpad.org/.

Blue, Kevin, and Ryan Craig. "Opinion: College Athletics Departments Do a Better Job Counseling Students than Career Offices." *The Hechinger Report*. February 5, 2019. http://hechingerreport. org/opinion-college-athletics-departments-do-better-job-counseling-students/.

Boettcher, Michelle et al. "The Cultivation of Support Networks by Students of Color in a Residence Hall Setting at a Predominantly White Institution." *Journal of College and University Student Housing* 45, no. 3 (2019): 30–46. https://eric.ed.gov/?id=EJ1220516.

Bond-Theriault, Candace. "14 Black LGBTQ+ Folks on How They're Taking Care of Themselves Right Now." *SELF*, June 26, 2020. https://www.self.com/story/black-lgbtq-self-care-tips.

"Book Argues that Mentoring Programs Should Try to Unveil Colleges' 'Hidden Curriculum.'" Accessed September 30, 2021. https://www.insidehighered.com/news/2014/08/04/book-argues-mentoring-programs-should-try-unveil-colleges-hidden-curriculum.

Boston College, Faculty Directory. "Andrés Castro Samayoa," n.d. https://www.bc.edu/bc-web/ schools/lynch-school/faculty-research/faculty-directory/andres-castro-samayoa.html.

Bowman, Nicholas A. "College Diversity Experiences and Cognitive Development: A Meta-Analysis." *Review of Educational Research* 80, no. 1 (2010): 4–33. https://doi. org/10.3102/0034654309352495.

Bradley, Rachel. "Measuring Self-Efficacy and Self-Regulation in Online Courses." *College Student Journal* 51 (2018).

Brady, Shannon T., Geoffrey L. Cohen, Shoshana N. Jarvis, and Gregory M. Walton. "A Brief Social-Belonging Intervention in College Improves Adult Outcomes for Black Americans." *Science Advances* 6, no. 18 (2020): eaay3689. https://doi.org/10.1126/sciadv.aay3689.

Brandon, A., J. B. Hirt, and Tracey Cameron. "Where You Live Influences Who You Know: Differences in Student Interaction Based on Residence Hall Design." *Journal of College and University Student Housing* 35 (2008): 62–79.

brightspot strategy. "How to Design Student Services for Non-Traditional Students" (blog). April 2, 2019. https://www.brightspotstrategy.com/student-support-services-design-equity/.

brightspot strategy. "How to Improve First-Gen Student Experience at Higher Ed Institutions." March 25, 2020. https://www.brightspotstrategy.com/first-generation-student-experience-higher-education/.

brightspot strategy. "Service: Student Journey Mapping." Accessed September 29, 2021. https:// www.brightspotstrategy.com/our-services/service-student-experience-snapshot/.

brightspot strategy. "Student Experience Strategy to Support Underserved Students." Accessed September 29, 2021. https://www.brightspotstrategy.com/whitepaper/support-underserved-higher-education-student-experience/.

Brown, Joshua, Fred Volk, and Elisabeth M. Spratto. "The Hidden Structure: The Influence of Residence Hall Design on Academic Outcomes." *Journal of Student Affairs Research and Practice* 56, no. 3 (2019): 267–83. https://doi.org/10.1080/19496591.2019.1611590.

Burns, Bridget, and Alex Aljets. "Using Process Mapping to Redesign the Student Experience." *Educause Review*, March 26, 2018. https://er.educause.edu/articles/2018/3/using-process-mapping-to-redesign-the-student-experience.

Campbell, Edward J. "Veteran Student Success: An Evaluation of Veteran Students' Perceptions of a Cohort Learning Model." PhD diss., Oregon State University, 2016.

"Campus Pride Index." Accessed September 30, 2021. https://www.campusprideindex.org/.

Cataldi, Emily Forrest, Christopher T. Bennett, and Xianglei Chen. "First-Generation Students: College Access, Persistence, and Postbachelor's Outcomes." US Department of Education (NCES 2018-421), February 2018).

Celestine, Nicole. "9 Strength Finding Tests and Assessments You Can Do Today," PositivePsychology.com. June 7, 2019. https://positivepsychology.com/strength-finding-tests/.

Center for First-Generation Student Success (website). Accessed September 30, 2021. https://firstgen.naspa.org/home.

Center for Self-Determination Theory. "Theory." Accessed September 29, 2021. https://selfdeterminationtheory.org/theory/.

"Center for the Study of HBCUs at VUU." Accessed September 30, 2021. https://center4hbcu.vuu.edu/.

Charli AI (website). Accessed September 29, 2021. https://www.charli.ai/.

Chavez, Alicia Fedelina. "Islands of Empowerment: Facilitating Multicultural Learning Communities in College." *International Journal of Teaching and Learning in Higher Education* 19, no. 3 (2007): 274–88.

Chen, Grace. "How Well Do Community College Students Perform after Transferring?" *Community College Review*, October 10, 2020. https://www.communitycollegereview.com/blog/how-well-do-community-college-students-perform-after-transferring.

Chiu, Joyce. "Why 89% of Companies Are Prioritizing Data Fluency" DataCamp. September 18, 2019. https://www.datacamp.com/community/blog/why-89-percent-of-companies-are-prioritizing-data-fluency.

Clark, Damon, David Gill, Victoria Prowse, and Mark Rush. "Using Goals to Motivate College Students: Theory and Evidence from Field Experiments." *The Review of Economics and Statistics* 102, no. 4 (2020): 648–63. https://doi.org/10.1162/rest_a_00864.

Clayton Smith, "International Student Success," *Strategic Enrollment Management Quarterly* 4, no. 2 (2016): 61–73.

Clockwise (website). Accessed September 29, 2021. https://www.getclockwise.com/.

"College Belonging: Dr. Terrell Strayhorn," *Just a Few Questions* (podcast), January 30, 2021. https://anchor.fm/marc-sims/episodes/College-Belonging-Dr--Terrell-Strayhorn-epn51c.

College Board. "Trends in College Pricing." Accessed September 30, 2021. https://research.collegeboard.org/trends/college-pricing.

Columbia University in the City of New York (website). International Students & Scholars Office. Accessed September 30, 2021. https://isso.columbia.edu/.

Conlin, Luke David, et al., "Guardian Angels of Our Better Nature: Finding Evidence of the Benefits of Design Thinking." ASEE Annual Conference & Exposition, June 14, 2015. https://peer.asee.org/guardian-angels-of-our-better-nature-finding-evidence-of-the-benefits-of-design-thinking.

Contreras-Mendez, Susana, and Lindsey Reichlin Cruse. "Busy with Purpose: Lessons for Education and Policy Leaders from Returning Student Parents." *IWPR* (blog), March 16, 2021. https://iwpr.org/iwpr-issues/student-parent-success-initiative/busy-with-purpose-lessons-for-education-and-policy-leaders-from-returning-student-parents/.

Coursicle (website). Accessed September 29, 2021. https://www.coursicle.com/.

Creative Reaction Lab. "A Method for Co-Creating Equitable Outcomes." Accessed September 29, 2021. https://www.creativereactionlab.com/our-approach.

Cress, Christine M. "Civic Engagement and Student Success: Leveraging Multiple Degrees of Achievement." *Diversity & Democracy* 15, no. 3 (2012). https://www.aacu.org/publications-research/periodicals/civic-engagement-and-student-success-leveraging-multiple-degrees.

Cruse, Lindsey Reichlin, Barbara Gault, and Jooyeoun Suh. "Time Demands of Single Mother College Students and the Role of Child Care in Their Postsecondary Success." *IWPR* (blog), May 10, 2018. https://iwpr.org/iwpr-general/time-demands-of-single-mother-college-students-and-the-role-of-child-care-in-their-postsecondary-success/.

Cui, Sheng, Yangyong Ye, and Xiaojing Zhang. "Uncovering the Sources of the Head Student Wage Premium – Based on China College Student Panel Survey." Hamburg, Germany: European Educational Research Association, 2019. https://eera-ecer.de/ecer-programmes/conference/24/contribution/47459/.

Daugherty, Lindsay, William R. Johnston, and Tiffany Berglund. "Connecting College Students to Alternative Sources of Support: The Single Stop Community College Initiative and Postsecondary Outcomes." RAND Corporation, April 29, 2020. https://www.rand.org/pubs/research_reports/RR1740-1.html.

del Rio, Lesley. "One Student Parent Shares the Impact of the Crisis."l *Imaginable Futures* (blog). Accessed September 30, 2021. https://www.imaginablefutures.com/learnings/guest-blog-one-student-parent-shares-impact-crisis/.

Desilver, Drew. "A Majority of U.S. Colleges Admit Most Students Who Apply." *Pew Research Center* (blog). April 9, 2019. https://www.pewresearch.org/fact-tank/2019/04/09/a-majority-of-u-s-colleges-admit-most-students-who-apply/.

Devlin, Ann Sloan, Sarah Donovan, Arianne Nicolov, Olivia Nold, and Gabrielle Zandan. "Residence Hall Architecture and Sense of Community: Everything Old Is New Again." *Environment and Behavior* 40, no. 4 (2008): 487–521. https://doi.org/10.1177/0013916507301128.

Do Good Work Educational Consulting (website). Accessed September 30, 2021. https://dogoodworkllc.org/team/

Do Good Work Educational Consulting. "Higher Ed Libs Faculty Office Hours." Accessed September 30, 2021. https://www.flipsnack.com/dogoodwork/whatworks-highered-libs-short-version.html.

"Do You Know Your Wellness Quotient™ Score?" Accessed September 30, 2021. https://www.surveymonkey.com/r/WellnessQuotientScore.

Duhigg, Charles. "How to Win Arguments Like an FBI Hostage Negotiator." *Slate*, September 27, 2020. https://slate.com/human-interest/2020/09/how-to-get-an-upgrade-tips-fbi-hostage-negotiator-chris-voss.html.

Dunn, Amina. "Younger, College-Educated Black Americans Are Most Likely to Feel Need to 'Code-Switch.'" *Pew Research Center* (blog). September 24, 2019. https://www.pewresearch.org/fact-tank/2019/09/24/younger-college-educated-black-americans-are-most-likely-to-feel-need-to-code-switch/.

Dweck, Carol. "The Power of Believing that You Can Improve." TEDxNorrkoping 1418832726, November 2014. https://www.ted.com/talks/carol_dweck_the_power_of_believing_that_you_can_improve.

EdSurge. "Want to Hire an Innovative College Graduate? Choose a Transfer Student." *EdSurge News*, June 2, 2021. https://www.edsurge.com/news/2021-06-02-want-to-hire-an-innovative-college-graduate-choose-a-transfer-student.

EducationData. "College Dropout Rates." Accessed September 30, 2021. https://educationdata.org/college-dropout-rates.

edX. "Communication Skills for Dialoguing across Difference." Accessed September 29, 2021. https://www.edx.org/course/communication-skills-for-dialoguing-across-difference.

Effective Change Agent. "Space Matters: Race, Equity and the PCC Landscape." Accessed September 29, 2021. https://ecapdx.weebly.com/space-matters-race-equity-and-the-pcc-landscape.html.

Ellett, Tom. "Masked and Engaged." Accessed September 30, 2021. https://www.insidehighered.com/views/2021/03/30/building-campus-culture-and-enhancing-student-experience-during-covid-19.

"Equitable Value Explorer," accessed November 30, 2021. https://www.postsecondaryvalue.org/equitable-value-explorer/

Equity in Mental Health Framework. "Recommendations for Colleges and Universities to Support the Mental Health of Students of Color." Accessed September 30, 2021 https://equityinmentalhealth.org.

Farmer-Hinton, Raquel L. "Social Capital and College Planning: Students of Color Using School Networks for Support and Guidance." *Education and Urban Society* 41, no. 1 (2008): 127–57. https://doi.org/10.1177/0013124508321373.

Felix, Elliot. "Five Ways to Better Support First-Generation Students" *brightspot strategy* (blog). March 25, 2020. https://www.brightspotstrategy.com/first-generation-student-experience-higher-education/.

Felix, Elliot, and Adam Griff. "Ending the Runaround: 12 Steps to Integrated Student Services." brightspot strategy. May 15, 2019. https://www.brightspotstrategy.com/integrated-student-services-best-practices/.

Fiorella, Logan, and Richard E. Mayer. "Role of Expectations and Explanations in Learning by Teaching." *Contemporary Educational Psychology* 39, no. 2 (2014): 75–85. https://doi.org/10.1016/j.cedpsych.2014.01.001.

First Generation Foundation. "Supporting First Generation College Students." Accessed September 30, 2021. http://www.firstgenerationfoundation.org/.

"First Year Experience, Persistence, and Attainment of First-Generation College Students." Washington, DC: RTI International, 2019. https://firstgen.naspa.org/journal-and-research/national-data-fact-sheets-on-first-generation-college-students/national-data-fact-sheets

Fishman, Tiffany, Jen Tutak, and Allan Ludgate. "Success by Design." Deloitte Insights. March 16, 2017. https://www2.deloitte.com/us/en/insights/industry/public-sector/improving-student-success-in-higher-education.html.

Forest (website). Accessed September 29, 2021, https://www.forestapp.cc/.

Freeman, Scott, Sarah L. Eddy, Miles McDonough, Michelle K. Smith, Nnadozie Okoroafor, Hannah Jordt, and Mary Pat Wenderoth. "Active Learning Increases Student Performance in Science, Engineering, and Mathematics." *Proceedings of the National Academy of Sciences* 111, no. 23 (2014): 8410–15. https://doi.org/10.1073/pnas.1319030111.

Friedman, Zack. "Student Loan Debt Statistics In 2021: A Record $1.7 Trillion." Forbes. Feburary 20, 2021. https://www.forbes.com/sites/zackfriedman/2021/02/20/student-loan-debt-statistics-in-2021-a-record-17-trillion/

Gallup, Inc. "The Gallup-Purdue Index 2015 Report." Accessed September 29, 2021. https://www.gallup.com/services/185924/gallup-purdue-index-2015-report.aspx.

Gallup, Inc. "StrengthsFinder 2.0." Gallup.com. Accessed September 29, 2021. https://www.gallup.com/cliftonstrengths/en/254033/strengthsfinder.aspx.

Gamboa, B. R. "Impact of Course Length on and Subsequent Use as a Predictor of Course Success." Crafton Hills College (report, RRN 788), November 8, 2013. https://www.craftonhills.edu/~/media/Files/SBCCD/CHC/About%20CHC/Research%20and%20Planning/Research%20Briefs/Academic%20Success%20Studies/Compressed%20Course%20Study.pdf.

Gault, Barbara, Lindsey Reichlin Cruse, Elizabeth Reynolds, and Meghan Froehner. "4.8 Million College Students Are Raising Children." *IWPR* (blog), November 17, 2014. https://iwpr.org/iwpr-issues/student-parent-success-initiative/4-8-million-college-students-are-raising-children/.

Generation Hope. "Resources and Workshops." Accessed September 30, 2021. https://www.generationhope.org/resources-workshops

Georgetown University Center on Education and the Workforce. "Ranking ROI of 4,500 US Colleges and Universities." Accessed September 30, 2021. https://cew.georgetown.edu/cew-reports/collegeroi/

Goldfarb, Anna. "The Right Way to Ask, 'Can I Pick Your Brain?'" *New York Times*, March 17, 2019. https://www.nytimes.com/2019/03/17/smarter-living/the-right-way-to-ask-can-i-pick-your-brain.html.

Goldrick-Rab, Sara, Christine Baker-Smith, Vanessa Coca, Elizabeth Looker, and Tiffani Williams. "College and University Basic Needs Insecurity: A National #RealCollege Survey Report," April 2019, 54. https://hope4college.com/wp-content/uploads/2019/04/HOPE_realcollege_National_report_digital.pdf.

Grant, Adam. "Think Again, the Latest Book from Adam Grant." September 22, 2020. https://www.adamgrant.net/book/think-again/.

Gross, Natalie. "From 'Boots to Books': How Tailored College Classes Help Vets in Transition." Reboot Camp, August 24, 2018. https://rebootcamp.militarytimes.com/news/education/2018/08/24/from-boots-to-books-how-tailored-college-classes-help-vets-in-transition/.

GroupMe (website). Accessed September 29, 2021. https://groupme.com/en-US/.

Guerra, Jennifer. "Teaching Students How to Switch between Black English and Standard English Can Help Them Get Ahead." State of Opportunity, July 16, 2014. https://stateofopportunity.michiganradio.org/education/2014-07-16/teaching-students-how-to-switch-between-black-english-and-standard-english-can-help-them-get-ahead.

Guiffrida, Douglas A., Martin F. Lynch, Andrew F. Wall, and Darlene S. Abel. "Do Reasons for Attending College Affect Academic Outcomes?: A Test of a Motivational Model From a Self-Determination Theory Perspective." *Journal of College Student Development* 54, no. 2 (2013): 121–39. https://doi.org/10.1353/csd.2013.0019.

Guttman Community College, Center on Ethnographies of Work. "Ethnographies of Work." Accessed September 29, 2021. https://guttman.cuny.edu/faculty-staff/center-on-ethnographies-of-work/ethnographies-of-work/.

Melanie Hanson, "College Dropout Rates [2021" Education Data (blog), November 22, 2021, https://educationdata.org/college-dropout-rates

Harvard University. "Group Work." Accessed September 29, 2021. https://bokcenter.harvard.edu/group-work.

Hawkins, Amy L. "Relationship between Undergraduate Student Activity and Academic Performance," *Purdue e-Pubs*, April 23, 2010, 41.

Hawkins, Catherine, Michael Smith, Raymond Hawkins, and Darlene Grant. "The Relationships among Hours Employed, Perceived Work Interference, and Grades as Reported by Undergraduate Social Work Students." *Journal of Social Work Education* 41 (2005): 13–27. https://doi.org/10.5175/JSWE.2005.200202122.

Hembree, Diana. "New Report Finds Student Debt Burden Has 'Disastrous Domino Effect' on Millions of Americans." Forbes. November 1, 2018. https://www.forbes.com/sites/dianahembree/2018/11/01/new-report-finds-student-debt-burden-has-disastrous-domino-effect-on-millions-of-americans.

Hendricks, Christina. "Renewable assignments: Student work adding value to the world" University of British Columbia, October 29th, 2015 https://flexible.learning.ubc.ca/news-events/renewable-assignments-student-work-adding-value-to-the-world/"Renewable assignments: Student work adding value to the world." University of British Columbia, October 29th, 2015 https://flexible.learning.ubc.ca/news-events/renewable-assignments-student-work-adding-value-to-the-world/

Hensly, Catherine, Chaunté White, and Lindsey Reichlin Cruse. "Re-Engaging Student Parents to Achieve Attainment and Equity Goals." IWPR (blog), July 8, 2021. https://iwpr.org/iwpr-issues/student-parent-success-initiative/re-engaging-student-parents-to-achieve-attainment-and-equity-goals/.

"High Graduation Rates for Community College Transfers." Inside Higher Ed. Accessed September 30, 2021. https://www.insidehighered.com/news/2012/11/08/high-graduation-rates-community-college-transfers.

Hinton, Corrine E. "'I Just Don't Like to Have My Car Marked': Nuancing Identity Attachments and Belonging in Student Veterans." *Journal of Veterans Studies* 6, no. 3 (2020): 84–100. https://doi.org/10.21061/jvs.v6i3.211.

Holden, Shelley L., Brooke E. Forester, Henry N. Williford, and Erin Reilly. "Sport Locus of Control and Perceived Stress among College Student-Athletes." *International Journal of Environmental Research and Public Health* 16, no. 16 (2019): 2823. https://doi.org/10.3390/ijerph16162823.

Hosick, Michelle. "NCAA Adopts Interim Name, Image and Likeness Policy." NCAA, June 30, 2021. https://www.ncaa.org/about/resources/media-center/news/ncaa-adopts-interim-name-image-and-likeness-policy.

Hrabowski, Freeman. "4 Pillars of College Success in Science." TED2013. 1365434089, February 2013. https://www.ted.com/talks/freeman_hrabowski_4_pillars_of_college_success_in_science.

Hyun, Jenny, Brian Quinn, Temina Madon, and Steve Lustig. "Mental Health Need, Awareness, and Use of Counseling Services Among International Graduate Students." *Journal of American College Health* 56, no. 2 (2007): 109–18. https://doi.org/10.3200/JACH.56.2.109-118.

Ideas. "The Impact of COVID-19 on the University Student Experience," February 3, 2021. https://www.wework.com/ideas/research-insights/research-studies/the-impact-of-covid-19-on-the-university-student-experience.

IIE. "Preparing to Study in the USA: 15 Things Every International Student Should Know." Accessed September 30, 2021. https://www.iie.org:443/en/Research-and-Insights/Publications/Preparing-to-Study-in-the-USA.

Indiana University. "NSSE's Conceptual Framework (2013)." Accessed September 29, 2021. https://nsse.indiana.edu//nsse/psychometric-portfolio/conceptual-framework-new-version.html.

Insel, Paul, and Walton Roth. "Levenson Multidimensional Locus of Control Scales: Wellness Worksheet 6." In *Core Concepts in Health*, 10th ed. McGraw-Hill, 2006. https://osf.io/h7sqj/download.

Institute for Women's Policy Research (website). Accessed September 30, 2021. https://iwpr.org/.

Intercultural Development Inventory. "The Roadmap to Intercultural Competence Using the IDI." April 10, 2012. https://idiinventory.com/.

Ithaka S+R. "New Report: Enrolling More Veterans at High-Graduation-Rate Colleges and Universities" (blog), January 10, 2019. https://sr.ithaka.org/blog/new-report-enrolling-more-veterans-at-high-graduation-rate-colleges-and-universities/.

IvyWise. "College Admissions Counseling." Accessed September 29, 2021. https://www.ivywise.com/.

IWPR. "Student Parent Success Initiative Archives" (blog). Accessed September 30, 2021. https://iwpr.org/category/iwpr-issues/student-parent-success-initiative/.

Jack Kent Cooke Foundation. "Persistence: The Success of Students Who Transfer from Community Colleges to Selective Four-Year Institutions." Accessed September 30, 2021. https://www.jkcf.org/research/persistence/.

Klein, Gary. "Performing a Project Premortem." *Harvard Business Review*, September 1, 2007. https://hbr.org/2007/09/performing-a-project-premortem.

Kuh, George D. "High-Impact Educational Practices." Association of American Colleges & Universities, June 24, 2014. https://www.aacu.org/node/4084.

Kuh, George. "What Student Affairs Professionals Need to Know About Student Engagement." *Journal of College Student Development* 50 (2009). https://doi.org/10.1353/csd.0.0099.

LaCosse, Jennifer, Elizabeth A. Canning, Nicholas A. Bowman, Mary C. Murphy, and Christine Logel. "A Social-Belonging Intervention Improves STEM Outcomes for Students Who Speak English as a Second Language." *Science Advances* 6, no. 40 (2020): eabb6543. https://doi.org/10.1126/sciadv.abb6543.

Lagesse, Austin. "Student-Athlete Career Success Stories." Bethel University Athletics. April 14, 2020. https://athletics.bethel.edu/news/2020/4/14/general-student-athlete-career-success-stories.aspx.

Lapinski, Zack. "America's Math Curriculum Doesn't Add Up (People I [Mostly] Admire, Ep. 42)." *Freakonomics* (blog). August 27, 2021. https://freakonomics.com/podcast/pima-math-curriculum/.

Lapsey, Daniel, Kenneth Rice, and Gregory Shadid, "Psychological Separation and Adjustment to College." *Journal of Counseling Psychology* 36, no. 3 (1989): 286–94. https://psycnet.apa.org/buy/1989-38171-001.

Learning and the Adolescent Mind. "Philip Uri Treisman." Accessed September 29, 2021. http://learningandtheadolescentmind.org/people_05.html.

Levenson, H. "Multidimensional Locus of Control in Psychiatric Patients," *Journal of Consulting and Clinical Psychology* 41 (1973): 397–404.

"Liberal arts education pays off in the long term, Georgetown report finds," January 17, 2020. https://feed.georgetown.edu/access-affordability/liberal-arts-education-pays-off-in-the-long-term-georgetown-report-finds/.

Linktree (website). Accessed September 29, 2021. https://linktr.ee/.

Lipson, Sarah Ketchen, Adam Kern, Daniel Eisenberg, and Alfiee M. Breland-Noble. "Mental Health Disparities Among College Students of Color." *Journal of Adolescent Health: Official Publication of the Society for Adolescent Medicine* 63, no. 3 (2018): 348–56. https://doi.org/10.1016/j.jadohealth.2018.04.014.

Lowe, Katie, and Travis Dorsch. "Parents of NCAA Student-Athletes: How Are They Involved and Does It Matter?" *Athletic Director U* (blog). September 24, 2019. https://athleticdirectoru.com/articles/does-parental-involvement-matter-ncaa-student-athletes/.

Lumina Foundation. "Today's Student." Accessed September 30, 2021. https://www.luminafoundation.org/campaign/todays-student/.

MacFarquhar, Larissa. "The Mind-Expanding Ideas of Andy Clark." *The New Yorker*, March 26, 2018. https://www.newyorker.com/magazine/2018/04/02/the-mind-expanding-ideas-of-andy-clark.

Mallinckrodt, Brent, and Sedlacek, William. "Student Retention and the Use of Campus Facilities by Race." *NASPA Journal* 46 (1987). https://doi.org/10.2202/1949-6605.5031.

Manno, Bruno. "Manno: College Is More than a Wage Premium — It's a Road to Well-Being and a Satisfying Life." August 4, 2019. https://www.the74million.org/article/college-is-more-than-a-wage-premium-its-a-road-to-well-being-and-a-satisfying-life/.

Marist College. "Center for Student-Athlete Enhancement." Accessed September 29, 2021. https://www.marist.edu/student-life/athletics/student-athlete-enhancement.

Marks, Jenna. "The Impact of a Brief Design Thinking Intervention on Students' Design Knowledge, Iterative Dispositions, and Attitudes towards Failure." PhD diss., Columbia University, 2017. 10274661.

Mason, Kisha. "2021 Report on Employer Views of Higher Education." Association of American Colleges & Universities, March 30, 2021. https://www.aacu.org/2021-report-employer-views-higher-education.

McCluney, Courtney L., Kathrina Robotham, Serenity Lee, Richard Smith, and Myles Durkee. "The Costs of Code-Switching." *Harvard Business Review*, November 15, 2019. https://hbr.org/2019/11/the-costs-of-codeswitching.

"The Mental Health Cost of Code-Switching on Campus." *Teen Vogue*, September 11, 2019. https://www.teenvogue.com/story/the-mental-health-cost-of-code-switching-on-campus.

Michigan State University. "Student Parent Resource Center Offers Wealth of Resources." *MSUToday*. September 1, 2021. https://msutoday.msu.edu/news/2021/student-parent-resources.

Mind Tools. "SMART Goals: How to Make Your Goals Achievable." Accessed September 29, 2021. http://www.mindtools.com/pages/article/smart-goals.htm.

Mitola, Rosan, Erin Rinto, and Emily Pattni. "Student Employment as a High-Impact Practice in Academic Libraries: A Systematic Review." *Journal of Academic Librarianship* 44, no. 3 (2018): 352–73. https://doi.org/10.1016/j.acalib.2018.03.005.

Morris, Amanda, and Emily Anthes. "For Some College Students, Remote Learning Is a Game Changer." *New York Times*, August 23, 2021. https://www.nytimes.com/2021/08/23/health/covid-college-disabilities-students.html.

Morsy, Sara. "Data-Driven Methods for Course Selection and Sequencing." PhD diss., University of Minnesota, 2019. https://conservancy.umn.edu/bitstream/handle/11299/206428/Morsy_umn_0130E_20206.pdf.

"The Most Ethnically Diverse National Universities in America." *USNews*. Accessed September 30, 2021. https://www.usnews.com/best-colleges/rankings/national-universities/campus-ethnic-diversity.

Museus, S. D., Yi, V., & Saelua, N. "How Culturally Engaging Campus Environments Influence Sense of Belonging in College: An Examination of Differences Between White Students and Students of Color." *Journal of Diversity in Higher Education* 11, no. 4 (2018): 467–83. https://doi.org/10.1037/dhe0000069.

Museus, Samuel D., and Kathleen M. Neville. "Delineating the Ways that Key Institutional Agents Provide Racial Minority Students with Access to Social Capital in College." *Journal of College Student Development* 53, no. 3 (2012): 436452. doi:10.1353/csd.2012.0042.

NASPA Center for First-Generation Student Success. "National Data Fact Sheets." Accessed September 30, 2021 https://firstgen.naspa.org/journal-and-research/national-data-fact-sheets-on-first-generation-college-students/national-data-fact-sheets.

National Association of Colleges and Employers. "Trends Continue for Career Services' Location, Reporting Structure." October 4, 2019. https://www.naceweb.org/career-development/trends-and-predictions/trends-continue-for-career-services-location-reporting-structure/.

National Center for College Students with Disabilities (website). Accessed September 30, 2021. https://www.nccsdonline.org/.

National Center for Education Statistics, IPEDS Trend Generator. "Number of people employed by postsecondary institutions" excluding "Instructional" occupational category. Accessed September 30, 2021.

National Center for Education Statistics. "Characteristics of Postsecondary Students." Accessed September 30, 2021. https://nces.ed.gov/programs/coe/indicator/csb?tid=74.

National Center for Education Statistics. "Digest of Education Statistics, 2020." Accessed September 29, 2021. https://nces.ed.gov/programs/digest/d20/tables/dt20_317.10.asp?currentyes.

National Center for Education Statistics. "NCES Fast Facts: Graduation Rates." Accessed September 30, 2021. https://nces.ed.gov/fastfacts/display.asp?id=40.

National Center for Education Statistics. "NCES Fast Facts: Students with Disabilities." Accessed September 30, 2021. https://nces.ed.gov/fastfacts/display.asp?id=60.

National Institute for the Study of Transfer Students (website). Accessed September 30, 2021. https://www.nists.org.

National Student Clearinghouse Research Center. "Tracking Transfer," September 23, 2021. https://nscresearchcenter.org/tracking-transfer/.

"New ACE Report Outlines Strategies for Supporting International Students Throughout Lifecycle." February 12, 2021. https://www.acenet.edu/News-Room/Pages/ACE-Report-Outlines-Strategies-for-Supporting-International-Students.aspx.

Niche. "2022 Best College Dorms in America." Accessed September 30, 2021 https://www.niche.com/colleges/search/best-college-dorms/

North Carolina State University Libraries. "Technology Lending." Accessed September 29, 2021. https://www.lib.ncsu.edu/devices.

O'Hara, Ross E. "Supporting Student Parents' Success in College." *Psychology Today*, July 7, 2020. https://www.psychologytoday.com/us/blog/nudging-ahead/202007/supporting-student-parents-success-in-college.

OFFTIME. "OFFTIME App. Unplug, It's Enough." Accessed September 29, 2021. https://offtime.app/index.php.

Osei, Zipporah. "Visions of a Post-COVID Higher Education Utopia." *Open Campus* (blog). April 24, 2020. https://www.opencampusmedia.org/2020/04/24/visions-of-a-post-covid-higher-education-utopia/.

PACER's National Parent Center in Transition and Employment. "Stories." Accessed September 30, 2021. https://www.pacer.org/transition/stories/.

Pappano, Laura. "College Chatbots, with Names Like Iggy and Pounce, Are Here to Help." *New York Times*, April 8, 2020. https://www.nytimes.com/2020/04/08/education/college-ai-chatbots-students.html.

Parker, Kim, Nikki Graf, and Ruth Igielnik. "Generation Z Looks a Lot Like Millennials on Key Social and Political Issues." *Pew Research Center's Social & Demographic Trends Project* (blog), January 17, 2019. https://www.pewresearch.org/social-trends/2019/01/17/generation-z-looks-a-lot-like-millennials-on-key-social-and-political-issues/.

Pascarella, Ernest T., Tricia A. Seifert, and Charles Blaich. "How Effective Are the NSSE Benchmarks in Predicting Important Educational Outcomes?" *Change: The Magazine of Higher Learning* 42, no. 1 (2010): 16–22. https://doi.org/10.1080/00091380903449060.

Patterson, Ransom. "The 25+ Best Productivity Apps in 2021." College Info Geek. October 18, 2019. https://collegeinfogeek.com/productivity-apps/.

Payscale. "Best Value Colleges." Accessed September 30, 2021. https://www.payscale.com/college-roi

Penn State University. "Disability services staff help remove barriers for students to be successful," July 27, 2020. https://news.psu.edu/story/626762/2020/07/27/impact/disability-services-staff-help-remove-barriers-students-be-successful

Pettigrew, Thomas, and Linda Tropp. "How Does Intergroup Contact Reduce Prejudice? Meta-Analytic Tests of Three Mediators." *European Journal of Social Psychology* 38 (2008): 922–34. https://doi.org/10.1002/ejsp.504.

Porter, William L. "Designers' Objects." In Design Representation, edited by Gabriela Goldschmidt and William L. Porter, 63–79. London: Springer, 2004. https://doi.org/10.1007/978-1-85233-863-3_3.

Postsecondary National Policy Institute. "Veterans in Higher Education," November 9, 2019. https://pnpi.org/veterans-in-higher-education/.

Powell, Farran, and Emma Kerr. "How to Find and Secure Scholarships for College." *US News & World Report*. February 5, 2020. https://www.usnews.com/education/best-colleges/paying-for-college/articles/how-to-find-and-secure-scholarships-for-college.

Puzio, Angelica. "Who Wants to Return to the Office?" FiveThirtyEight. August 11, 2021. https://fivethirtyeight.com/features/why-post-pandemic-offices-could-be-whiter-and-more-male/.

Redden, Elizabeth. "International Student Well-Being." *Inside Higher Ed*. May 31, 2019. https://www.insidehighered.com/news/2019/05/31/panel-focuses-mental-health-needs-international-students.

Remind (website). Accessed September 29, 2021. https://www.remind.com/.

Rhodes, Dawn. "Black Studies Struggle at State Universities under Current Fiscal Climate." *Chicago Tribune*, September 6, 2016. https://www.chicagotribune.com/news/breaking/ct-african-american-studies-college-major-met-20160905-story.html.

Richman, Mike. "Navigating the College Experience." US Department of Veterans Affairs, October 6, 2017. https://www.research.va.gov/currents/1017-Veterans-face-challenges-in-higher-education.cfm.

Rodriguez, Sarah L., et al., "Inclusion & Marginalization: How Perceptions of Design Thinking Pedagogy Influence Computer, Electrical, and Software Engineering Identity." *International Journal of Education in Mathematics, Science, and Technology* 8, no. 4 (2020). *https://www.ijemst.org/index.php/ijemst/article/view/952*.

Rutgers Center for Minority Serving Institutions (website). Accessed September 30, 2021. https://cmsi.gse.rutgers.edu/.

Sax, Linda J., and Katherine Lynk Wartman. "Studying the Impact of Parental Involvement on College Student Development: A Review and Agenda for Research." In *Higher Education: Handbook of Theory and Research*, edited by John C. Smart, 25:219–55. Dordrecht: Springer Netherlands, 2010. https://doi.org/10.1007/978-90-481-8598-6_6.

Jeff Selingo, Who Gets In and Why: *A Year Inside College Admissions* (New York: Scribner, 2020), 55.

Selingo, Jeff, and Michael Horn. "What's Going on with the Workforce." *Future U* (podcast, Ep. 89). October 25, 2021. https://www.futureupodcast.com/episodes/whats-going-on-with-the-workforce/.

Sheriff, Sarah. "Social Change Model of Leadership Development." Dickinson College. Accessed September 30, 2021. https://www.dickinson.edu/info/20380/student_leadership/3795/social_change_model_of_leadership_development.

Shift (website). Accessed September 29, 2021. https://tryshift.com/.

Silver, Blake R. The Cost of Inclusion: *How Student Conformity Leads to Inequality on College Campuses* (University of Chicago Press, 2020).

Soria, Krista. "Advising Satisfaction: Implications for First-Year Students' Sense of Belonging and Student Retention." *The Mentor: an Academic Advising Journal* 14 (2012). https://doi.org/10.26209/mj1461316.

Soria, Krista M., Jan Fransen, and Shane Nackerud. "The Impact of Academic Library Resources on Undergraduates' Degree Completion." *College & Research Libraries* 78, no. 6 (2017). https://doi.org/10.5860/crl.78.6.812.

Spacefinder (website). Accessed September 29, 2021. https://spacefinder.lib.cam.ac.uk/.

Spanierman, Lisa B., Jason R. Soble, Jennifer B. Mayfield, Helen A. Neville, Mark Aber, Lydia Khuri, and Belinda De La Rosa. "Living Learning Communities and Students' Sense of Community and Belonging." *Journal of Student Affairs Research and Practice* 50, no. 3 (2013): 308–25. https://doi.org/10.1515/jsarp-2013-0022.

SRLS Online. "Socially Responsible Leadership Scale." Accessed September 29, 2021. https://srls.umd.edu/.

Steelcase, Inc. "Steelcase Report: 5 Key Findings around Employee Engagement." Accessed September 29, 2021. https://info.steelcase.com/global-employee-engagement-workplace-comparison.

Sternin, Jerry, Richard T. Pascale, and Sternin, Monique. *The Power of Positive Deviance*. Harvard Business Press, 2010.

Strayhorn, Terrell. *College Students' Sense of Belonging: A Key to Educational Success for All Students*. Routledge & CRC Press, 2019.

Student Veterans of America (website). Accessed September 30, 2021. https://studentveterans.org/.

Student-Athlete Insights (website). Accessed September 29, 2021. https://studentathleteinsights.com.

"Students with depression twice as likely to drop out of college," Michigan News, July 10, 2009, https://news.umich.edu/students-with-depression-twice-as-likely-to-drop-out-of-college/

Sullivan, Katie, and Kay Yoon. "Student Veterans' Strengths: Exploring Student Veterans' Perceptions of Their Strengths and How to Harness Them in Higher Education." *Journal of Continuing Higher Education* 68, no. 3 (2020): 164–80. https://doi.org/10.1080/07377363.2020.1806013.

Talks at Google. "Chris Voss: Never Split the Difference," 2016. https://www.youtube.com/watch?v=guZa7mQV1I0.

TechCrunch. "A New App Called Moment Shows You How Addicted You Are to Your IPhone." Accessed September 29, 2021. https://social.techcrunch.com/2014/06/27/a-new-app-called-moment-shows-you-how-addicted-you-are-to-your-iphone/.

The Ezra Klein Show. "Wilco's Jeff Tweedy Wants You to Be Bad at Something. It's for Your Own Good." *The New York Times*, July 2, 2021, https://www.nytimes.com/2021/07/02/opinion/ezra-klein-podcast-jeff-tweedy.html.

The Hope Center. "Research." Accessed September 29, 2021. https://hope4college.com/research-and-resources/research/.

The Posse Foundation. "The Posse Veterans Program." Accessed September 29, 2021. https://www.possefoundation.org/shaping-the-future/posse-veterans-program.

The U Experience (website). Accessed September 29, 2021. https://www.theuexperience.com.

Thielking, Megan. "A Dangerous Wait: Colleges Can't Meet Soaring Student Needs For Mental Health Care." *STAT*. February 6, 2017. https://www.statnews.com/2017/02/06/mental-health-college-students/.

Townsend, Sarah S. M., Nicole M. Stephens, and MarYam G. Hamedani. "Difference-Education Improves First-Generation Students' Grades Throughout College and Increases Comfort with Social Group Difference." *Personality and Social Psychology Bulletin* 47, no. 10 (2021): 1510–19. https://doi.org/10.1177/0146167220982909.

"Two Indicators: Women and Work." NPR, September 17, 2021. https://www.npr.org/transcripts/1038307729.

Tynan, Dan. "How Academic Centers Help Student-Athletes Hit Peak Performance." *EdTech*, February 21, 2019. https://edtechmagazine.com/higher/article/2019/02/how-academic-centers-help-student-athletes-hit-peak-performance.

Tyson, Charlie, "The Hidden Curriculum," Insider Higher Ed, August 4, 2014, https://www.insidehighered.com/news/2014/08/04/book-argues-mentoring-programs-should-try-unveil-colleges-hidden-curriculum.

United Negro College Fund. "Student Pulse Survey: COVID-19 Impact on Fall 2020 Educational Plans." July 2020. https://uncf.org/wp-content/uploads/UNCF-Student-Pulse-Survey-Results_Final.pdf.

University of California San Francisco Student Disability Services (website). Accessed September 30, 2021. https://sds.ucsf.edu/home.

University of Kentucky. "Academic Coaching Student Testimonials." Accessed September 30, 2021, https://www.uky.edu/acadcoach/student-testimonials.

University of Massachussetts Amherst. "The Stonewall Center." Accessed September 30, 2021. https://www.umass.edu/stonewall/.

University of Michigan, LSA Inclusive Teaching. "Social Identity Wheel." n.d. https://sites.lsa.umich.edu/inclusive-teaching/social-identity-wheel/.

University of Minnesota. "Evaluation Shows U of M Student Parent HELP Centers' Positive Effects on Undergraduate Student Parent Academic Outcomes." *News and Events*, July 31, 2021. https://twin-cities.umn.edu/news-events/evaluation-shows-u-m-student-parent-help-centers-positive-effects-undergraduate-student.

University of Minnesota. "University Services – Study Space." Accessed September 29, 2021. https://studyspace.umn.edu/.

University of Missouri–St. Louis. "Madison's Success Story." Accessed September 30, 2021. https://www.umsl.edu/studentadvocacy/studentparents/madison.html.

University of Rochester. "Izone." Accessed September 29, 2021. https://izone.lib.rochester.edu/.

University of South Carolina. "National Resource Center for the First-Year Experience and Students in Transition," Accessed September 30, 2021 https://sc.edu/about/offices_and_divisions/national_resource_center/index.php.

University of Washington. "Managing Imposter Syndrome: Husky Experience Toolkit." Accessed September 30, 2021. https://sas.uaa.uw.edu/husky-experience/know-yourself/managing-imposter-syndrome/.

US Department of Education. "College Scorecard." Accessed September 30, 2021. https://collegescorecard.ed.gov/

US Department of Education, Federal Student Aid. "FAFSA® Application." Accessed September 29, 2021. https://studentaid.gov/h/apply-for-aid/fafsa.

US Department of Veterans Affairs. "Find a Yellow Ribbon School." Accessed September 30, 2021. https://www.va.gov/education/yellow-ribbon-participating-schools/

US Department of Veterans Affairs. "VA College Toolkit: Services." Accessed September 30, 2021. https://www.mentalhealth.va.gov/student-veteran/services.asp.

US Department of Veterans Affairs. "VetSuccess on Campus." Accessed September 30, 2021. https://www.benefits.va.gov/vocrehab/vsoc.asp.

US Government Accountability Office. "Higher Education: Students Need More Information to Help Reduce Challenges in Transferring College Credits." August 14, 2017. https://www.gao.gov/products/gao-17-574.

Virginia Commonwealth University. "Military Student Services." Accessed September 30, 2021. https://militaryservices.vcu.edu/.

Wallace, David Foster. "This Is Water – Full Version – David Foster Wallace Commencement Speech." YouTube, 2013. https://www.youtube.com/watch?v=8CrOL-ydFMI.

Wang, Jing, and Jonathan Shiveley. "The Impact of Extracurricular Activity on Student Academic Performance." January 2009, 19. Available at https://www.cair.org/wp-content/uploads/sites/474/2015/07/Wang-Student-Activity-Report-2009.pdf

Wesaw, Alexis, Kevin Kruger, and Amelia Parnell. "Landscape Analysis of Emergency Aid Programs." July 5, 2016. https://www.naspa.org/report/landscape-analysis-of-emergency-aid-programs.

Wesley, Alexa, Alexis Wesaw, and Omari Burnside. "Employing Student Success: A Comprehensive Examination of On-Campus Student Employment." NASPA report, February 15, 2019. https://www.naspa.org/report/employing-student-success-a-comprehensive-examination-of-on-campus-student-employment.

Wikimedia Foundation. "Implementation Intention." June 23, 2021. https://en.wikipedia.org/w/index.php?title=Implementation_intention&oldid=1030077453.

Wikimedia Foundation. "Volatility, Uncertainty, Complexity and Ambiguity." Accessed September 30, 2021. https://en.wikipedia.org/wiki/Volatility,_uncertainty,_complexity_and_ambiguity.

Wikimedia Foundation. "Wicked Problem." Accessed September 30, 2021. https://en.wikipedia.org/wiki/Wicked_problem.

Wilder Foundation. "University of Minnesota – Student Parent Help Center," May 8, 2020. https://www.wilder.org/wilder-research/research-library/university-minnesota-student-parent-help-center.

Young, Sharon. "Veterans Adjustment to College: Construction and Validation of a Scale." *Journal of Veterans Studies* 2 (2017): 13. https://doi.org/10.21061/jvs.13.

Zhao, Chun-Mei. "Achieving Multicultural Competence: Student Participation in College Activities and Its Impact on Multicultural Learning David Cheng," vol. 21. Citeseer, 2005. https://citeseerx.ist.psu.edu/viewdoc/download?doi=10.1.1.561.8402&rep=rep1&type=pdf.

Made in USA - North Chelmsford, MA
1299177_9781735810768
01.19.2022 0911